D0283114

EXIT

STRATEGY

. . . .

Thinking Outside the Box

EXIT
STRATEGY
·····························
Thinking Outside the Box

Michelle Cromer

JEREMY P. TARCHER/PENGUIN
a member of Penguin Group (USA) Inc.
New York

JEREMY P. TARCHER / PENGUIN
Published by the Penguin Group
Penguin Group (USA) Inc., 375 Hudson Street, New York, New York 10014, USA
Penguin Group (Canada), 90 Eglinton Avenue East, Suite 700, Toronto, Ontario
M4P 2Y3, Canada (a division of Pearson Penguin Canada Inc.)
Penguin Books Ltd, 80 Strand, London WC2R 0RL, England
Penguin Ireland, 25 St Stephen's Green, Dublin 2, Ireland (a division of Penguin Books Ltd)
Penguin Group (Australia), 250 Camberwell Road, Camberwell, Victoria 3124, Australia
(a division of Pearson Australia Group Pty Ltd)
Penguin Books India Pvt Ltd, 11 Community Centre, Panchsheel Park,
New Delhi–110 017, India
Penguin Group (NZ), Cnr Airborne and Rosedale Roads, Albany, Auckland 1310,
New Zealand (a division of Pearson New Zealand Ltd)
Penguin Books (South Africa) (Pty) Ltd, 24 Sturdee Avenue, Rosebank,
Johannesburg 2196, South Africa

Penguin Books Ltd, Registered Offices: 80 Strand, London WC2R 0RL, England

Most Tarcher/Penguin books are available at special quantity discounts for bulk purchase for
sales promotions, premiums, fund-raising, and educational needs. Special books or book
excerpts also can be created to fit specific needs. For details, write Penguin Group (USA) Inc.
Special Markets, 375 Hudson Street, New York, NY 10014.

Library of Congress Cataloging-in-Publication Data

Cromer, Michelle, date.
    Exit strategy : thinking outside the box / Michelle Cromer.
        p.   cm.
    ISBN 1-58542-505-2
    1. Death care industry—United States.   2. Funeral rites and ceremonies—United States.
I. Title.
    HD9999.U53U5257   2006   2006044499
    338.4'7393—dc22

Printed in China
10 9 8 7 6 5 4 3 2 1

Book design by Laura Lindgren

For Barry,

for our boys,

August and Sam,

and

in memory of Catalina

C O N T E N T S

ACKNOWLEDGMENTS

My first thanks go to Francine Maroukian: if it were not for you and your idea to make a chapter into a book, I would not have written *Exit Strategy.*

Charles Burkhalter, my great friend and agent, thank you for selling me, a first-time author, and this book to the second-largest publishing company in the world.

Ken Siman, my editor at Tarcher/Penguin, thank you for agreeing to meet me for breakfast in May 2003, and for all of your advice on the publishing world. Thank you for believing in me, for your wise words, and for your constant help. I will never forget what you have done for me.

To Laura Lindgren, Ken Swezey, David Pfendler, thanks for bringing your vast professional talents to my team. A huge *"Muchas gracias"* to John Strausbaugh for sharing your brain with me and for teaching me how to write a good book on time, with passion.

Thanks to all the people I interviewed, especially Beth Menczer, Jay Murphy, Don Brawley, George Frankel, and

Corky Ra. And to Norma Garber and Kristen and Jessica Jernigen for sharing such personal moments with me.

Of my friends and family who allowed me to stay with them or share a meal as I traveled to interviews, I thank Carolyn and Ron Smith, Garry Kershaw, Cathy and Drew Rosen, Christopher Barbour, Jonathan Gibbs, and in particular my father-in-law, Jim Cromer, who let me stay in Naples twice, flew to Key West for my interview, paid for everything, and threw two fabulous dinner parties, of course.

I have many friends to thank. Park Kerr, for introducing me to Francine. Perla Maldonado, for being with me at the beginning of this journey, and for our friendship. Rhonda Dore, for telling me to just write like I talk—great advice. Alice White and Amy Hussmann, for sharing your father's story and for all the phone calls, wine, and encouragement. Bob Wingo, my friend and business partner, for teaching me how to think outside the box for twenty years. Soffia Wardy, Valorie Montoya, Julian Garcia, Toni Dake, Tim and Patti Gallegly, Ron and Debbie Vernon, Monte and Shannon Batson, Nancy Cromer, Ron Fritsch, Carlos Veytia, Marc Beaudin, Edie Correa, and Jeri Baker. And Lupita and Ludy, for picking up my cleaning, the boys, the slack, and my spirit.

To my parents, Jim and Jenny Batson, thanks for giving me my work ethic and for teaching me that a soul is not something you have, it is what you are. And to Felicia Hopkins, thanks for nurturing my soul every Sunday.

My boys, August and Sam, thank you for understanding that I am not a conventional mother and for being so smart and so kind. I am proud of you both.

And to my husband, Barry: I could not have written this book without you. I am grateful for your patience, support, friendship, loyalty, and love. I am forever changed because of who you are and what you mean to me. *Con amor, siempre tuya.*

INTRODUCTION

On September 5, 2001, my son Sam was born, prematurely and as sick as could be. His nurse, who had evidently honed her bedside manner at a Marine boot camp, flatly told me that he wasn't going to live. A priest giving last rites to the baby next to him took one look at Sam and asked if I wanted him to give Sam last rites, too.

Death is not something I had thought about a great deal. My parents are still living, as are all of my siblings; at the time, so were all of my friends. As for me, I was healthy and had no intention of dying anytime soon, thank you. But as the hours stretched into days and then weeks and Sam continued to struggle for life, the death of a loved one became something I had to confront seriously for the first time.

Sam made it out, Nurse Ratched got fired, and I started to do a great deal of thinking about death and dying. My friends' parents began to pass away, and as I went to their funerals I noticed that there was something unique about each ceremony. In our parents' day, all funerals were pretty much the same, because grief-stricken families usually left matters to the funeral director and the minister, priest, or rabbi to do the organizing and set the tone. Everything was done according to tradition and ritual. What I noticed now was that my friends were taking more of a hand in crafting the ceremony, giving each loved one's send-off an individual flair and personal meaning.

Leave it to my generation, the baby boomers, to take control. We're not only organizing our parents' funerals, but even planning our own in advance, putting our requests in writing and letting everyone know exactly what we want. We're a demographic so totally accustomed to center stage that we will never give it up without some fanfare. I first noticed this in Lawrence Kasdan's 1983 homage to my generation, *The Big Chill.* After the priest announces that a college friend will play one of the deceased's favorite songs, JoBeth Williams's character, Karen, solemnly sits down at the church organ and hits the classic opening chords of the Rolling Stones' "You Can't Always Get What You Want." As that sixties anthem accompanied the funeral procession, I wasn't the only boomer in the audience who thought, *Now that's the way to go out.* In 2005, Hunter S. Thompson, legendary gonzo journalist and counterculture hero of my generation, even left behind a demand for his ashes to be shot out of a cannon—a plan made possible by his friend Johnny Depp, the actor who portrayed Thompson in the film version of his famous book *Fear and Loathing in Las Vegas.*

With baby boomers pushing up the average age in the United States, "death care" has grown into a $16 billion industry since the mid-1980s, a trend expected to continue through 2012. It has also been consolidating, as corporate chains have bought up some 20 percent of the nation's funeral homes, with the rest remaining independent and family-run, like the one in *Six Feet Under.*

Whereas the vast majority of their parents simply put themselves and their loved ones in the hands of their local funeral director when the time came, boomers are taking a much more active role in the planning. And when members of the biggest consumer-driven generation in history pick up their platinum cards and commence to plan their own funerals with the kind of verve and zeal once reserved for prom night, you can bet that boomers are causing not just growth but change in the funeral business. This trend—referred to as "self-planning"—is widespread and growing. For the first time in their industry's history, the nation's 25,000 funeral directors have to think about how to "market" themselves to us. They're offering us choices and options in everything from casket styles to burial sites, disposal of cremated remains, and a variety of personalized funeral and memorial services.

Because I'm a planner by nature—I don't leave the drive-way without an agenda and a map—I started to think ahead to my own passing. I hope that's far in the future, but I figure it's never too early to start shopping around. I began to research my options, and *Exit Strategy* shows the results. As I traveled around, I found people all over the United States exploring new, creative alternatives to traditional funeral and burial practices. I found that cremation, an option chosen by only about 5 percent of Americans thirty years ago, is a growing trend. I talked to visionary businesspeople and artists who will shoot my cremated remains into space, pack me into a golf club, mummify me, or turn me into a one-carat diamond (a choice so irresistible I have decided to make my husband, Barry, into a fabulous bracelet . . . someday). I met families whose loved ones had conscientiously planned in advance to become part of an eco-friendly reef or forest, part of a growing "green burial" movement. I interviewed people who will be deep-frozen when they die, gambling that, at some point in the future, medical science will be able to revive them. Asking our parents what they want has become polite dinner conversation.

Whatever options people were exploring, it was clear to me that the opportunity to carry out their own and their loved ones' personal exit strategies can be a deeply moving and emotionally satisfying experience. Death becomes less cold and impersonal, which makes it easier to see it as part of the eternal cycle of life.

I hope that *Exit Strategy* inspires you to think outside the box about how you want to go when the time comes—to look ahead to the inevitable not with "fear and loathing" but with a plan and a purpose. After all, it's your funeral. Why let strangers make the arrangements?

EXIT
STRATEGY
. . . .
Thinking Outside the Box

UNCLE ERNIE

CHAPTER ONE

❋

Feats of Clay

"I don't do it every day, mind you," Beth Menczer says, "but ever since I made my father into a flute for my mother, well, it just opened up a whole new world."

Beth Menczer is a clay artist. She throws, sculpts, fires, and exhibits. More than that, she makes human remains into pieces of art.

Beth's mother actually thought of mixing cremated ashes with potter's clay to make a lasting piece of art. "Shortly after my father died, my mother said, since volcanic ash was used from prehistoric to pueblo potters to give strength to the clay, why can't human ashes be used?"

Coming from a family of artists, Beth never stopped to think that this might be strange. "My father found out he had pancreatic cancer and knew that was a death sentence. He pleaded with his doctors not to do chemo. They told him he would only live three months. He wasn't afraid to die.

"Death is very much a part of life on a ranch," Beth continues. "Kids on a ranch or a farm learn early on that animals die all the time. Death is not something to fear. We're all going to die. Kids today may see a pet die, but that's about it. That's why I think there's so much fear surrounding death in this country."

Beth lives in New Mexico, "the land that Georgia O'Keeffe painted." A petite, dark-haired, beautiful woman, she lives among chickens, roosters, geese, dogs, cats, and horses. Add all the wildlife that abounds in that part of the country, and it's easy to see where she gets inspiration for her clay animals.

Typically, Beth's sculpting process begins with collecting the clay, which she gathers from the Zuni pueblo in Pilar, New Mexico, and from her home in Glenwood. "I walk around, looking for clay on the ground. I pick up the clay I think might work, and noodle it and roll it around to make sure it won't crack. If it doesn't crack, that means the clay has elasticity, and I need that to sculpt."

Carbon dating of ancient Indian pots traces the art back to 30,000 B.C., long before recorded history. Most of our knowledge of the first American Indians is based on their clay work alone; fired clay is the only material on earth that does not change with time. Historians generally believe that fired clay pottery developed because ancient people lined their woven

2

baskets with mud clay. When the baskets were subjected to fire, so that corn or other food could be dried, the baskets burned, leaving the hard, durable clay intact.

Beth's brother Kenny, also a potter, added the cremated ashes of their father to the clay Beth had already gathered. They both created objects. Using the same technique as his sister, Kenny made bowls and sculptural pieces that were distributed to family members.

"We fired the pieces outdoors, using cow patties as fuel," he explains.

That was more than ten years ago. Beth has continued to create vessels for grieving family and friends, wedging the ashes into clay and making something unique for each occasion.

"I have to meet or at least speak with a close friend or relative of the deceased," she says. "They have to bring the person back to life with stories, tell me about special interests and what he or she was like. I usually get an idea right away of what I would like to create, but I keep the ashes in my home for a while, until the idea congeals. It's a very intimate process."

Torie, a recent client of Beth's, tells me her story. When Torie's father died of pancreatic cancer, she, her husband, and her mother sat down with Beth and talked about him.

"On the day he died, my husband and I were getting ready for bed when I heard an owl. I opened up the blinds, and there was the owl, sitting on a flagpole that was lit by a spotlight along a six-lane highway. As I sat there, the owl hooted nine times, and each time he hooted he looked over to the window. It was such an unlikely event that I knew Dad—who loved owls—had sent it. And the message to me from Dad was, 'Don't worry. Yes, I am very much alive. There is another realm, and all is well.'

"So an owl was the logical choice for Beth to make," Torie says. "I got chills, and tears came to my eyes when I saw it. It brought me back to the night when my dad sent us that owl messenger."

Beth says that handling a person's ashes is a huge responsibility. "This was a person. I never forget that." One to two cups of sifted ashes go into each piece of pottery. Any ashes left over can be given back to the family, but in most cases the family allows Beth to plant the remaining ashes under one of her forty-eight beautiful rosebushes.

With the ashes mixed in, Beth wets the clay and places it on a plaster slab. Then she kneads it and begins molding the piece.

How long does it take?

"A lifetime," Beth says of her pieces. "It takes all of my life experience to make each piece."

WHY CREMATE?

In his encyclopedic book *Death to Dust,* Dr. Kenneth V.
Iserson explains that cremation has been used since prehistoric
times, and in many cultures it has been preferred over burial.
It is even required in Buddhism and Hinduism. The ancient
Greeks believed that burning the body freed the soul. In
ancient Rome, cremation was considered more honorable than
burial, which was reserved for "murderers, suicides, and individuals who died after being struck by lightning (since they
were thought to be cursed by Jupiter)." Because the Greeks,
Romans, and other "pagans" cremated their dead, the ancient
Hebrews shunned the practice, although the Bible tells us that
the bodies of Saul and his sons were burned. To this day, cremation is not allowed for Orthodox Jews.

As Christianity became dominant, cremation all but disap-
peared in Western societies, because Christians believe that the
body will be resurrected when Christ returns to earth. Since
the beginning of the twentieth century, however, it has gradually lost the stigma it once had, although it's still frowned on by
some churches. In England and Europe, where available land
for burials is scarce, roughly 70 percent of the deceased are

low cremated. The figures are much lower in the United States. Still, over the last thirty years, the number of Americans choosing cremation over burial has dramatically increased. In 1975, only about 5 percent of the deceased in the United States were cremated. By 2002, according to the Cremation Association of North America, the number rose to almost 30 percent, and CANA predicts that by 2025 it will be nearing 50 percent.

Nowadays, any funeral home director will help make the arrangements with a reputable crematorium. Since a crematorium in Georgia made headlines a few years ago for mishandling and mixing up cremated remains, or cremains, CANA and funeral directors around the country have implemented a number of guidelines and controls to ensure that the ashes you are handed are indeed your loved one's.

There are several reasons why more and more people are choosing cremation. It can be far less expensive than a traditional burial, with a simple cremation costing under $1,000, as opposed to the average $6,500 for conventional funeral and burial services. Many people believe that, from the environmental perspective, it is preferable to taking up land in large cemeteries. And as American society has become highly mobile and families more far-flung, gravesite visits can be impractical and inconvenient. It's much easier for family members to keep

Cremation is simple and efficient. Our bodies are mostly water and soft tissue, which evaporate in the fire; what's left of the average adult is four to eight pounds of ashes and small bone fragments. Some people say they're surprised to see how coarse cremains are; they expected to see a fine powder, like what's left in an ashtray. Many people keep the cremains of their loved ones in urns, which they either have in their homes or place in special buildings at cemeteries called columbaria. But Americans are now choosing a wide variety of other ways to preserve or dispose of cremains.

CHAPTER TWO

✦

The Final Flight Plan

I stepped out of a coffee shop in Seattle and overheard a local say, "The mountain's out." I had been to Seattle many times, but it always had been characteristically cloudy. But on this bright, sunny, gorgeous day, the 14,410-foot Mount Rainier unveiled herself in all her dazzling geological glory, dominating the landscape. I stared in such reverence, wondering if I should bow to this volcanic goddess. The proud local— actually, now I think back on it, the *possessive* local—shared with me that Mount Rainier is so big, it has its own weather system.

Mount Rainier provides one of the magnificent backdrops for the cremains-scattering flights of Jim and Wendy Howard's Aerial Missions in Seattle, Washington. For $295, they fly within a twenty-five-mile radius of their base, which allows them to spread the ashes over the extraordinary natural beauty that surrounds Seattle—the mountains, lakes, forests, and the waters of Puget Sound.

Jim became interested in flying back in 1987, when he was working in a lumberyard in upstate New York. "The owner had a seaplane, which he used to deliver blueprints and check on the camps that he was building in the Adirondacks," he recalls. "He also had four sons who had their pilot's licenses. One of the sons, Scott, asked me if I wanted to go up one day. And that's all it took."

Jim obtained his own pilot's license. A few years later, he heard from Scott, who had moved to Seattle to fly seaplanes. At Scott's urging, Jim earned the necessary instrument and commercial pilot ratings, and in 1995 he moved to Seattle. When I spoke with him, he had logged more than 5,800 hours of flight time.

Jim bought a Cessna 170, the plane used by the California Highway Patrol. "It must be a good plane—why else would they use it?" As luck would have it, he found a beautifully restored 1956 model right in his own backyard, near Mount Rainier. It's in this plane that he and Wendy perform the aerial scattering of ashes.

"I am the son of a United Church of Christ minister," he explains. "When he died, he requested to be cremated. As a family we scattered his ashes around a lake in the Adirondacks, because he loved it there. We traveled the lake by boat and left some of his ashes at many of his favorite spots. What a wonderful tribute to a human being. It felt to me like we were setting a human soul free."

"I decided to do ash-scattering with my plane to offer a service to people while still doing something I enjoy," Jim says. He got a license from the state to perform the service, and set up his Web site. "That's how most people find us, through our Web site."

Although entire families come to Seattle for the service, only one or two people can go up with Jim and Wendy in the small plane for the actual release of the ashes.

"We strongly encourage a family member or close friend to come up with us to witness the scattering," Jim says. "And we can perform a flyover with the ashes, so the people on the ground can witness the scattering." Sometimes a family will charter another plane to fly alongside Jim's, so that more of them can be closer to the scattering. Jim says his clients rarely want any kind of formal ceremony to go along with the scattering. "Usually the people who come up with us are just absorbed in their own thoughts."

Not everyone feels the need to be present for the service, however. Sometimes the survivors simply send the ashes to Jim. They need to declare at their post office that they are shipping human cremains, which get special handling and are sent by registered mail. Jim sends back a notarized certificate within

11

twenty-four hours of the service, noting the date, time, and place of the scattering.

Jim has his own technique for scattering the ashes. Before taking off, he carefully places the ashes in what looks like a wind sock, which he hands to a family member. When the Cessna arrives at the proper location, they hand the ashes back to Jim. He extends the sock out his window, where it unfurls and gradually releases the cremains.

"It's beautiful, really," he says.

He remembers a couple in their fifties who came up from Oklahoma to scatter the cremains of the woman's mother. "The woman kept saying over and over that she just wanted to be able to see Mount Rainier. But it was a cloudy day in Seattle and we couldn't see it. So I worked the plane through the hills, and finally found a hole in the clouds and went through it. And there was Mount Rainier in all her glory. The only way to describe it was euphoric."

The Native Americans who live here tell the story of how the great goddess Tahoma, whose name means "the mountain who was God," grabbed her child and left her husband while he was going through a fit of jealous rage. Tahoma stretched her neck and looked back so many times along the way that she grew enormously tall. She finally stopped her flight a hundred miles southeast of Seattle. And that is where she stands today, providing a magnificent setting for Jim's missions.

It's no surprise that Mount Rainier has inspired many myths and legends among the people who have lived in its awesome presence. Rainier is the tallest of a chain of volcanoes in the region, and it has been said that there are "lakes of fire" near its peak. Frontiersmen claimed there were giants living in the mountain's caves and caverns, and according to some, the spirits of elk gods roam its snowy flanks.

CHAPTER THREE

❀

Dazzling Particles of Light

One of the things I love about living on the Texas–Mexico border is that I can be standing in the United States one minute, and in a Third World country the next. It's just a short walk across a bridge from El Paso into the city of Juárez. My husband and I often make the trip on Saturday afternoons. We stroll to the colorful Mercado de Juárez, pull up a chair in a cantina, order cold bottles of Tecate beer, and marvel at the local artisans, who excel in the art of glassblowing. Juárez is world-famous for its beautiful handblown glassworks. I never tire of studying the men's dark eyes and the intense expressions on their worn faces as they lean over their fires, using the flames the way a painter uses his brushes to shape and form their work. As the delicate shapes and swirling colors emerge from the flames, you can see that each piece is as unique as the man who creates it.

Far away in Hinsdale, Illinois, Companion Star Crystal and Memorials creates glassworks that are even more rare. The company will take a small amount of a loved one's cremated remains and blow them into a one-of-a-kind glasswork in the shape and color of your choice.

"The whole point of my company is to think of people in light, rather than in darkness," founder Phyllis Janik explains. It was with this thought that she named her company. "Although the night sky reveals countless stars appearing to us as single, isolated entities," she has written, "most stars have one or more companions. They're separated by such vast distances that each is invisible to the other. Yet from where we stand, the star and its companions are one, and they perform a single dance of light."

Glass is made of sand, mixed with various minerals and metals, and forged and shaped at high heat. It's not known for certain when humans first began to fashion it. Glass beads, the simplest forms, were found at archaeological sites in the Near East and have been dated to roughly 4,500 years ago. I remember from Sunday school that glass is compared to gold in the Book of Job—the oldest book in the Bible, thought to have been written more than 3,500 years ago. The ancient Egyptians knew how to make beads, small bottles, and figurines of glass, and how to make colors by mixing in different metals. But they did not know how to blow glass into larger shapes, something that seems to have been developed in Syria around the first century A.D.

16

The old men in the Juárez market tell me a legend about the discovery of glass. It seems an ancient Phoenician merchant ship was crossing the Mediterranean with a cargo of soda when the crew disembarked on a small island and lit fires on the beach to cook their dinner. The island was all sand, with no stones to support their pots, so they used some blocks of soda from the ship. As the soda heated, it mixed with the sand and streams of a mysterious liquid flowed: glass.

Of course, the men who told me this story were drinking another kind of liquid, so who knows? I do know that glassblowing furnaces are stoked to temperatures much hotter than a campfire on a beach. And that it wasn't ancient Phoenicians, but Spanish conquistadors in the early 1500s, who brought the knowledge of glassblowing to Mexico.

The idea behind Companion Star came to Phyllis after the death of her father. "My father did *not* want to be boxed," she says, laughing. One day she was looking at a design for a glasswork she had drawn years before, and suddenly thought about having some of her father's ashes blown into the glass.

"My dad and my uncles worked in steel mills," Phyllis says. It occurred to her that steelmaking and glassblowing had a lot in common. "I thought that forging basic earth elements into glass was like the way basic elements are forged and changed through heat in the steelmaking process."

Phyllis gave the design to a glass artist, who made the commemorative piece for her. She had no intention of continuing

17

the process after that. She was busy teaching creative writing and literature at Moraine Valley College, in a suburb of Chicago, which she had done for thirty-three years. "After seeing what I had done with my dad, people kept asking me to do the same thing for them," she says.

After a great deal of research, Phyllis formed Companion Star. Since then, hundreds of people all over the country have had glass memorials made for loved ones (and pets) who have been cremated. They simply send a small amount of the cremains to the company and choose the basic design of the artwork from the wide variety shown on the company's Web site. There are solid spheres and egg-shaped sculptures of crystal-clear glass with swirls of iridescence dancing in their hearts. One sculpture is reminiscent of the owl-shaped urns in which the ancient Egyptians placed remains; another is adorned by a Greek dolphin. Or you can choose from smaller pendants and beads in a range of shapes, and in colors from a deep, opalescent black to a pastel amethyst. For the larger sculptural pieces, the company can also supply a pedestal that lights them from below, to breathtaking effect.

Phyllis points out that since each piece is individually crafted, and each incorporates a unique individual's ashes, no two are alike. Each piece forms its own patterns and hues in the forging; each catches and reflects light in its own way. In keeping with the company's theme, the designs have names that remind us of the glittering points of light in the night sky:

Nebula, Nova, Pulsar, Sirius. It's an acknowledgment, Phyllis says, that while these people have moved on from the physical plane, their light remains in our lives.

It generally takes six to eight weeks to receive your completed work of art. Prices begin at $175.

What's true of cremated remains in general certainly applies to these works of art: they're a much more convenient way for far-flung families to cherish loved ones' memories than the traditional grave site.

"As a matter of practicality, none of my family goes to a cemetery," Phyllis tells me. "My one surviving aunt, out of thirty-two aunts and uncles, is eighty-four and doesn't drive, so she can't get to a cemetery. My cousins are all scattered, my sister is in another state, and my daughter is in another state. I don't have time to drive two hours to our family cemetery myself."

Through Companion Star, each family member can actually *wear* their loved one as a beautiful piece of jewelry. Seeing the tiny specks of ash swirled inside the glass, playing forever in the light, they may think of that person every time they look up and gaze at the stars.

CHAPTER FOUR

◎

Gone Fishin'

In a perfect world, I would have three perfect jobs: snowboarding, fly fishing, and golfing. In the winter of 1999, I decided to put down my snow skis and take up snowboarding. I traveled to Powder Mountain in Utah to learn the sport. As anyone would, I kept tumbling and tripping the first couple of days. After one particularly bad fall, a young male snowboarder, maybe seventeen years old, stopped to help me up. I graciously accepted his assistance—until he said, "Wow, I think it's cool an old lady like you is snowboarding." A string of colorful words tumbled, tripped, and fell out of my old lady's mouth, and right then I decided to try that much harder.

I took up fly fishing after I saw the movie *A River Runs Through It.* When I participate in this quiet, graceful sport, it's the only time I allow myself to turn off my cell phone and my brain.

And then there's golf. There is only one way to describe my feeling for golf: passion. I either passionately hate it or passionately love it, and flip between those emotions from one stroke to the next.

It would be impossible for me to choose which of these three sports I like the best. And now, thanks to Rena Fregosi and David Riccomi, I don't have to. Their Creative Cremains company, based in San Francisco, will pack your ashes into shotgun shells, fishing rods, golf clubs, and any other kind of sporting equipment you could think of. And jewelry, musical instruments, books, artwork . . . Anything that can hold a person's ashes, really.

Plus, they'll sculpt you custom urns in all sorts of shapes. One of their clients, an avid sailor, now resides in an urn shaped like a sailboat. Another, who was a big hockey fan, rests in one shaped like the Stanley Cup.

"I want to be a totem pole," Rena tells me. And David wants to be put in a fishing pole. "We'll hollow out the handle, put David in there, seal it up, and David gets to fish forever," she explains. You can also have your pet's cremains placed in an urn sculpted to resemble the pet.

Asked how she got started in this business, Rena replies, "I have lost a lot of folks in my life." Twenty-five years ago, Rena's husband died, at the age of twenty. She's also lost her grandparents, her mother, and recently her stepfather. When her daughter went off to college, Rena decided to go back to school.

"I wanted to become a funeral director because of the experience I had with death. I thought I could help others," she says.

In the meantime, Rena was working for one of her late husband's best friends, David Riccomi. "David and I have been friends since we were seventeen. I was exploring what I wanted to do. I would go to work and share news stories with David. One story that caught my eye was about a man in England who put his cremains into an egg timer that he left to his wife as a tongue-in-cheek joke because she couldn't boil an egg."

Rena and David laughed over the story, but it got them thinking. David's background was in contracting, and Rena says she's a people person, "so it was a nice fit." He persuaded her to give up the funeral-director idea and go into business with him.

"It took us about a year," she recalls, to get the company rolling. "We kept everything under wraps and trademarked the name and did a great deal of research. David's shop in the city is our workshop. We don't have a showroom or urns on a shelf. People find us on our Web site."

Their first customer was Rena's mother. "I had her on my shelf for five years," Rena says. She told her sisters and stepfather she wanted to use her mother's ashes, and got permission from all of them. She didn't want to share exactly what she was going to do.

"My mom was known for her frog collection, so we used those that I could hollow out and fill up. We put her ashes in them and gave them to my sisters and her grandchildren. So now everyone has a piece of Mom they can take with them."

Let's say I tell my family I want my ashes packed into my favorite golf club when I go. They'd ship the club to Creative Cremains, where David and Rena would hollow it out. The family could also send my ashes, but Rena says, "We prefer to modify the object and ship it back, so the survivors can be a part of the process by putting in the cremains and sealing it up themselves. We recommend that they take the object to their local funeral home and allow the folks there to help."

As for those custom-made urns, Rena and David put a lot of care into assuring that each one is a truly unique and personalized resting place. Take the one shaped like a sailboat. That man's son "promised his father on his deathbed that he would fulfill his last wishes of being in an urn on his boat. We replicated the exact boat that the mom and dad lived on for ten years. He loved sailing into the wind, so I researched—because I didn't know—what kind of rudder to use. I went to yacht shows and picked up brochures to make sure everything was perfect."

When she had done all that homework, Rena took the plans to one of the sculptors she and David work with. "I work with fabulous artists. They understand they're working for the family. It is not the artist's project, it's the family's."

David crafted the stand so that the urn is tilted like a boat sailing into the wind. Rena fashioned the sails, and went to hobby shops to find the perfect anchor.

When the son took the finished product to his mother in Arizona, "she was dumbfounded," Rena proudly says. "She loved it. Every morning she comes downstairs and says hello."

In our highly mobile society, many people are seeing urns as preferable to traditional burial. "Everyone is in transit these days," Rena observes. "If you move, you aren't able to go visit the gravesite. So these pieces bring a lot of peace, because you take them with you. And it's artwork, not just a regular old ugly urn. This is artwork that will be passed down through the generations."

Because Creative Cremains matches each custom urn to the right artist, prices vary (based on a rate of seventy-five dollars an hour) and are of course discussed in advance.

"This is my perfect job," Rena says.

I'm glad someone has found one. I'm still trying to figure out how to combine my passions into a career. But at least now I know that when I go, I can be *gone fishin'* forever.

DID YOU KNOW?

 On average, right-handed people live nine years longer than the left-handed.

 People fear spiders more than they do dying. However, statistically you are more likely to be killed by a flying champagne cork than by the bite of a poisonous spider.

 Cockroaches can live for nine days without their heads, at which point they die of starvation.

 About one hundred people choke to death on ballpoint pens each year.

 The word *morgue* comes from the name of the building in Paris where bodies were laid out for identification. In the 1800s, the Paris morgue drew huge crowds of tourists—as many as 40,000 a day—for whom viewing dead bodies was a popular pastime. It was closed to the public in 1907.

 Caskets are not the same as coffins. Caskets are simple rectangles, whereas traditional coffins are wider at the shoulders and narrow at the feet. Today, caskets have almost entirely replaced coffins in use.

CHAPTER FIVE

Going Out Like a Viking

On the turquoise waters off the shores of Key West, Christy Barbour stands on the ledge of a thirty-two-foot Grand Banks trawler, silhouetted by the pink and orange hues of the sunset lighting up the southern sky. From the upper deck, Captain Jay Murphy respectfully asks, "Does this place feel right to you?" Which is code for "Are you emotionally ready to do this?"

Christy opens the black box that contains the ashes of her father. She stands silently for a moment as Captain Murphy points the classic wooden boat upwind. Dipping into the box, she sprinkles the powdery gray cremated remains over the waters. She watches solemnly as they form an undulating film and slowly drift with the current. Within moments, "in a concert of movement and emotion," as Captain Murphy says, Christy's father has become one with the sea.

Each of the six members of the Barbour group steps up and tosses a single red rose onto the waves, and they all say their last good-byes. Captain Murphy leads them in a traditional English burial prayer. After the group has had time to take photos and share stories, the trawler makes one last circle of the flowers, and then slowly heads back to shore.

Families choose scattering their loved ones' ashes at sea for many reasons. The deceased may have been a lover of the sea, for instance. Others choose it because it's environmentally friendly. It's also very affordable: Captain Murphy charges just $500 for a maximum party of six, and even provides drinks. He also gives the family an eleven-by-seventeen nautical chart marking the area where the ashes were released—latitude and longitude, sea state and direction of tide. Flowers and clergy are available on request.

The tradition of burial at sea is an ancient one, a practice that has been in existence as long as people have gone to sea. The Egyptians sent their dead out to sea, and over the centuries naval ships far from land on fighting missions have often used the world's oceans as watery cemeteries.

The Vikings are probably the culture we most associate with sea burials. I fell in love with Tony Curtis as he and the beautiful Janet Leigh stood on the shore, watching the lifeless body of Kirk Douglas honorably being lowered into his vessel and pushed out to sea in the 1958 movie *The Vikings.* Hundreds of burning arrows were shot into the boat as the horns sounded, sending Douglas into the afterlife. An ending fit for the Viking warrior he was.

Or at least an ending fit for the Hollywood interpretation of a Viking funeral. It is speculated that depending on the social status of the deceased Viking, large to small boats and everything in between were launched into sea with dead bodies aboard. The sea held such importance to the Vikings not only because it was their source of food; the oceans were their highways of commerce, bringing all kinds of items to help enrich, shape, and change their lives and culture. Ships were so strongly associated with the continuance of life that they were the natural choice for the vehicle in which to send off a Viking to his afterlife. The ship symbolized rebirth, a way for the Viking to defeat death and venture onward to whatever lay in the beyond.

At fifty-five, Captain Murphy looks like a Viking—or at least Hollywood's version of one—with his steely blue eyes and graying hair. In 2002, he sailed out of Boston's Winthrop marina and headed south. Thirty days later, he reached Key West, his new home.

"I designed computer circuit boards for a living, but my hobby was restoring old wooden boats. I decided to become a commercial fisherman, which I did for eleven years. I began to do ash scatterings at sea in Boston, for about three years, when I decided I needed a change," he explains. "My mind is at peace when I'm on the ocean. It's a perfect cure for ADD," he says, smiling.

In Key West, Captain Murphy takes charters out, in addition to doing ash scatterings. For the latter, he works with local funeral directors, but mostly, he says, "people find me from my Web site."

"I tell the families they're connecting with their loved one every time they swim," Captain Murphy continues. "I encourage them to honor their loved ones by returning to the sea on the anniversary. I don't think people ever die, really," he adds softly. "Especially if we keep them in our thoughts."

NOTABLE BURIALS AT SEA

Ingrid Bergman
1915–1982

Robert Mitchum
1917–1997

Rock Hudson
1925–1985

Steve McQueen
1930–1980

Jerry Garcia
1942–1995

Janis Joplin
1943–1970

John F. Kennedy, Jr.
1960–1999

CHAPTER SIX

◎

Sleep in the Deep

A six-foot-four, 350-pound, sixty-six-year-old man with a totally shaved head is used to being the center of attention in any room he enters. Today is no exception for Stephen Jay Garber. Except today, Steve is dead.

On this gorgeously warm January day in Sarasota, Florida, Steve's ashes, along with those of seven other people, are going to become part of something called Eternal Reefs. It's a man-made reef constructed out of large concrete modules, called reef balls, that are placed on the ocean floor to help rebuild natural reefs that have been eroded by mankind's presence or by severe weather.

Standing in front of rows of these modules, I can't help thinking of four-foot, 4,000-pound cupcakes, standing on their heads, with big Swiss-cheese holes punched through them. Yet these giant concrete cupcakes can withstand hurricane-force swells and last up to five hundred years. The holes are designed to attract fish, which can find shelter from storms or predators inside. The balls' rough surface allows coral, sponges, and other plants to adhere and flourish.

Depending on size, the balls cost $1,995 to $4,995, or cremated remains can be mixed together into a "community reef" for $995. Eternal Reefs can build a memorial reef in someone's honor, with or without the cremated remains. Pets' cremains also can be included.

"Steve was the first president of our Rotary Club in Lakewood Ranch, Florida," his friend Jerry Hearn explains. He describes Steve as a "big, brilliant teddy bear. He would always be the center of attention, but not ever wanting to be."

Neighbor and fellow Rotarian Jeff Travis went fishing with Steve on a regular basis. "Steve was not very good at doing nothing," he says, smiling, "and wasn't very good at letting me do nothing."

"Steve died the day before Christmas, of inoperable pancreatic cancer," Norma, his wife of forty-two years, tells me. Her blue eyes fill with tears. "It was a college romance, one of those that stayed together. We had a wonderful, wonderful life together."

Norma says Steve loved boating and fishing in Sarasota Bay, and that's the reason we're here. Steve and Norma heard about Eternal Reefs because they were both Parrot Heads—members of the nationwide network of Jimmy Buffett fans, headquartered in Atlanta. Parrot Heads are more than just a music fan club. Each local club is designed to get active and do charity work in their community. Becoming part of Eternal Reefs and helping to restore a bit of the ocean's ecosystem is a way for Steve to stay active even after death.

Eternal Reefs cofounder George Frankel is a former rafting guide now in his mid-forties. George tells me, "I have always been in love with the environment," he says. "I take a look every day at what this company's contribution is, and I am more and more enthralled with it."

Don Brawley, president of the company, is a former computer programmer. He's known George since high school. Don got the idea for this novel version of burial at sea from his father-in-law, who, after being diagnosed with cancer, asked for his cremated remains to become a part of a reef ball. "I'd rather spend eternity down there, with all that life and excitement going on, than in a field with dead people," Don remembers him saying.

Putting on diving gear and going to visit his late father-in-law's reef is a joyous experience that brings tears to Don's eyes. "The best feeling you're going to get from a cemetery is a somber one, at least for me," he says. "But when you go to visit a memorial reef and see the fish swimming and all the other sea life, you get a good feeling." He calls Eternal Reefs the "only death-care option that is truly an environmental contribution and also creates a permanent, living memorial for the deceased and their families."

The company, working with federal, state, and local governments, has created man-made reefs in approved environmentally challenged sites in locations from Ocean City, New Jersey, and the Chesapeake Bay to Sarasota and Pensacola in Florida to the Gulf shores of Texas. When I visited, more than three hundred people's ashes had become part of this magnificent project, with thousands more signed up.

Today, we're witnessing the first step of the process: the casting of the concrete balls. First, friends and family place their loved ones' ashes in buckets, where they mix them with water—and many a tear. This mixture is then poured from the buckets into the concrete and stirred in. We watch as the wet concrete is poured into large molds and cast into shape. After about a half hour, the balls are formed enough for family and friends to place their hands on them, or to write little messages in the still-moist surface.

"We wrote one word on our mother's reef," Kristen Jernigan tells me. She and her sister, Jessica, had come to Eternal Reefs at the request of their mother, who died of breast cancer. She loved the water and the idea of becoming part of a reef when she died. That word? *Belief.*

The balls are left in the open air to cure for a month. Then everyone is invited back to participate in the final step of the process. The balls are carefully loaded onto a barge, which is towed out to the reef site. Lowered to the seafloor by crane, the balls are guided into place by scuba divers.

As their loved one's reef ball is lowered into the sea, friends and family gather at one end of the boat to watch and share quiet time. Flowers that have been placed inside the balls float to the surface. The deceased's name is read as the ship's horn sounds.

"It was beautiful," Kristen Jernigan recalls. "For us Jernigans, we really feel like the reef is a completion of the circle of life for my mom. She's leaving something physical behind that so many will benefit from—and she's back in the ocean, a place she loved. Carrying our her final wishes and having a beautiful place to visit when we want to be near her ashes is a gift."

"Steve is now part of a fishing environment," Norma says. "I can now look out into the bay and know where he is. I am even buying a GPS unit so I can keep track of him. He's part of my living style as well as the environment. He would have liked that."

"Entire families are now learning to scuba, so they can return and dive down to see the progress of the reef balls," George Frankel proudly says. "We get measurable growth on our reef balls in three to six months. This is a remarkable environmental contribution. We're enhancing the fisheries for both commercial and recreational usage. And we hope we're relieving stress on some of the other fishing and diving locations, just because now there are more choices to go to."

At the end of each ceremony, there's a reading of the words of John F. Kennedy, who said it best:

I really don't know why it is that all of us are so committed to the sea. . . . I think it's because we all came from the sea. . . . And it is an interesting biological fact that all of us have in our veins the exact same percentage of salt in our blood that exists in the ocean. And therefore we have salt in our blood, in our sweat, and in our tears. We are tied to the ocean, and when we go back to the sea—whether it is to sail or to watch it—we are going back from whence we came.

Gandhi

It took the largest extras call in cinematic history to re-create the funeral of Mohandas K. Gandhi (Ben Kingsley) in Richard Attenborough's glorious film biography, *Gandhi* (1982). The sequence was filmed on January 31, 1981, the thirty-third anniversary of the assassinated leader's funeral, and 200,000 of the 300,000 extras worked as volunteers. The scene opens with the somber sound of the tread of combat boots (marching in parade formation over streets strewn with flower petals). Our view of the funeral procession starts small, focusing on Gandhi's body as it rests on a gun carriage, covered by blankets of flowers. But as sitar music begins to swell, the camera slowly pulls back to reveal a field of mourners—as far as the eye can see.

✳

Four Weddings and a Funeral

It may lack the grandeur of costume-drama film funerals, but it's hard to beat the emotional power of that one simple funeral among all those weddings in Mike Newell's *Four Weddings and a Funeral* (1994). Set in a humble church on an appropriately gray day, the normally reticent Matthew (John Hannah) discloses the extent of his relationship with the flamboyant Gareth (Simon Callow) as part of his eulogy: "Perhaps you would forgive me if I turn from my own feelings to the words of another splendid bugger, W. H. Auden," he says, before giving a heart-wrenching recitation of the poet's "Funeral Blues."

✳

All That Jazz

"Live like you'll die tomorrow, work like you don't need the money, and dance like nobody's watching," Broadway legend Bob Fosse once said—a philosophy that infuses his semi-autobiographical musical *All That Jazz* (1979). In its grand finale, director Fosse choreographs his own funeral, starring his black-sequin-sporting stand-in character Joe Gideon (Roy Scheider).

As the scene opens, the nurse is prepping Gideon for heart surgery. But in Gideon's mind, he lets us see Angelique (the angel of death, played by one of Fosse's real-life loves, Jessica Lange) applying his stage makeup. After a Vegas-style production of the Everly Brothers classic "Bye Bye, Love" (including the poignant lyric "Bye-bye, my love, good-bye"), Gideon leaves the stage and runs into the audience, a group composed of his cheering family and friends. As he takes his bows, shaking hands and hugging those who have been spectators and participants in his life, we hear one of his wildly clapping Broadway backers enthusiastically say, "This must have cost a fortune."

✳

CHAPTER SEVEN

※

Act Two Will Begin
After a Brief Intermission

I hope the Alcor people aren't wearing tinfoil pyramids on their heads, I say to myself as I drive through Scottsdale, Arizona, on a beautiful spring morning. "What kind of people think they can cheat death—and actually want to?"

Alcor is located off Frank Lloyd Wright Boulevard, where there's no evidence of Wright's style. I pass fast-food places, malls, convenience stores, and a Lamborghini car dealership—oddly familiar surroundings for Alcor's highly unusual enterprise.

Diane Cremeens, a beautiful young black woman, graciously greets me at the glass front door, then locks it behind me. Her manner is cautious yet tender. Diane is the Alcor Life Extension Foundation membership services coordinator. She asks me to wait in the small, modest reception area. I sink down in one of the two large leather armchairs and wait for the tour.

On the opposite wall there's a gallery of about twenty photos, with small brass plates bearing each person's name and the dates of their "first life cycle," birth to death. I walk over to take a closer look and discover the photo of Ted Williams. Urban legend has it that Walt Disney is at Alcor. Not true. But Boston Red Sox Hall of Famer Ted Williams is, which prompted a fierce legal battle among his children and friends, some of whom were appalled that he was not traditionally buried. His son John Henry is also frozen at Alcor.

Diane emerges from her office with a packet full of information. I read that since Alcor was established as a nonprofit in California in 1972, sixty-seven "patients" have been placed in cryopreservation, and over 740 living members have signed up.

The theory of cryopreservation, or cryonics, was first promoted in the mid-1960s in a widely read book, *The Prospect of Immortality,* by physics teacher Robert Ettinger. Ettinger went on to form his own Cryonics Institute, headquartered near Detroit. Cryonics is basically a technique that freezes the body to a point where physical decay stops. The body is then held in this state of "cryonic suspension" in hopes that eventually medical technology will be developed to revive the person—*reanimation* is the term used. Today, of course, no such technology exists. You can decide if you would like to have your entire body frozen, or just your head and brain, which is called neuropreservation. The idea behind the latter is that someday medical science will have advanced far enough to grow your revived brain a new body.

46

Maybe Ben Franklin was foreseeing Alcor when he wrote in a letter to a friend in 1773, "I should prefer to an ordinary death, being immersed with a few friends in a cask of Madeira wine, until that time, then to be recalled to life by the solar warmth of my dear country!"

Alcor performed its first neuropreservation on July 16, 1976: Fred Chamberlain, Jr., Alcor's first member, a former Army officer who'd served in both world wars, and whose son Fred and daughter-in-law Linda founded Alcor. They were the ones who named the organization after a star, Alcor, a barely visible companion star of Mizar, in the Big Dipper's handle. Alcor has been used for centuries as a test for good eyesight. If you can see Alcor, you have excellent focus and vision. It seemed an appropriate symbol.

As I sit in the lobby, my reading is interrupted by the front door bell. An older man who could be Peter Lawford's twin bursts in. His deep blue eyes match his starched cotton polo shirt. His manners are as polished as his tanned skin; he looks like he's been standing on the deck of a sailboat his entire life. With his salt-and-pepper hair and Ralph Lauren style, it's clear that this man came by way of cathedrals, castles, and polo fields to this southwestern desert town.

"Hello, my name is Jack," he announces in a plummy British accent. "And this is Brandon. We've arrived for the tour."

Brandon is a towering young man, with hair dyed jet black and a milky complexion. His baggy sweats and shirt don't

47

disguise his perfectly sculpted frame. He calls to mind a young Elvis.

Jack St. Clair has been an Alcor member since 1996. Brandon is a prospective member. "I want all my friends to join," Jack declares.

Noting my surprise to be meeting an Englishman in Arizona, Jack explains, "I bought a house 1.4 miles from here. I wanted to be closer, but that is as close as I could get. I wanted to sleep here, but they wouldn't let me," he says, and laughs. "I wish I could live here!"

I don't understand why he makes such a point about proximity to the facility. Jack explains that the sooner an Alcor team can "take over" after you're pronounced dead, the faster your brain can be frozen. "Every second counts," he says, because brain cells start to die right away. He rolls up his Egyptian cotton sleeve to reveal bracelets on both wrists. Members wear these Medic Alert–type bracelets, as well as a dogtag and a wallet card, all with the express written admonition that no autopsy be performed in the event of death. "If I know I'm going to die, I will come to my house in Scottsdale and wait," Jack says.

I also meet Roy Hollis, an Alcor member since 1998. A computer programmer, he moved to nearby Phoenix fourteen years ago. He has two grown children and has been married for thirty years.

"My wife doesn't have a problem with this, but she doesn't

want to do it," he tells me. "My daughter might, which would be great."

Roy tells me that along with their bodies—or, as in his eventual case, heads—Alcor provides storage for boxes of members' memorabilia, things they'll enjoy seeing and touching when they're reanimated someday in the future. "I'm going to set up a video camera and record memories," Roy says. I ask him what he thinks he'll miss most about this "first life cycle" when he's awoken in the future. "Me," he replies. "My whole body. And I'll miss connections to the people I love." Asked why he chose neuropreservation, he says, "I look at the brain as a big electronic device, and there's a disk drive that's storing information. I think when you die a switch goes off, and then when you're reanimated the switch comes back on."

A young blond appears and introduces herself as Tanya Jones, Alcor's chief operating officer. With her petite frame, short hair, and wire-rimmed glasses, she looks like she'd be more comfortable in a library than as the COO of such an organization. Tanya has been involved with Alcor for more than sixteen years. As she commences the tour, she speaks slowly and clearly, with a smile. It feels like a tour of an art gallery, not a building full of preserved humans.

She begins with that wall of photos. We learn that the oldest person Alcor has placed in suspension was a coal miner who died at ninety-nine, and that an entire family of four generations from Spain are members. The first in their family to

49

become a patient was the least likely—a woman of only twenty-one, who was murdered. Her great-grandmother joined her in suspension shortly after.

Tanya escorts us to the operating room, which has the standard look and feel—sterile, harsh, cold, everything chrome or white. Here she explains the cryonics process in great medical detail. Since I can go woozy at the site of a scratch, her explanation is way too graphic for me. Yet she delivers it dispassionately, as though telling us a recipe for Hamburger Helper.

As Jack said, Alcor's goal is to reach a member as quickly as possible after death, to begin the process immediately and preserve as many healthy cells as possible. Ideally, Alcor's team is on site at pronouncement of death. "There's only a six-to-twelve-minute window in order to preserve the patient," Tanya explains. The team quickly cools the body to −230 degrees Fahrenheit. Once that temperature is reached, the patient is brought down more gradually to −320 degrees, the temperature of liquid nitrogen.

Tanya explains the pros and cons of whole-body preservation versus neuropreservation. The neuro option is the most popular, she says, by a factor of four to one, not only because it's cheaper, but because many cryonics believers think the chances of reanimation are better. They predict that by the time medical science can reanimate a cooled-down brain, they will also have figured out how to grow that brain a brand-new body. The problem with preserving your whole body is that not only the brain, but all your other organs as well will have to be revived, not to mention repairing the body of whatever killed it in the first place.

Brandon announces that he doesn't want the body of an old person. "I want the body I have right now, today," he almost shouts. And who can blame him?

Tanya explains that you fill out a form where you can stipulate the type of body you want—tall, petite, blond, brunette, whatever. The way Alcor figures it, by the time your brain can be loaded into a newly grown body, genetic engineering will have progressed far enough that they can make you any kind of body you want. Including a replica of his current physique for Brandon.

"We are working to solve everything with regards to cryo-protection, the storage and revival," she says. "What we don't have control over is when they're going to cure cancer or old age."

The biggest concern in cryogenics today is ice damage, which ruptures cells. "Every single person who is cryo-preserved today has ice damage," Tanya concedes. One critic has famously argued that a thawed brain would look like a mush of strawberry jam. Although Alcor claims that it has per-fected methods for reducing this damage to the minimum, they're candid enough to admit that successful reanimation will require sophisticated cell repair technology. They're currently banking on advances in nanotechnology to do the job. Accord-ing to Alcor, experts estimate that it will be anywhere from twenty to a hundred years before the technology is available.

I ask Tanya if any research has been conducted on animals, freezing them and bringing them back. She admits that no one has accomplished this yet. "However," she adds, "we are hitting the edge of what we can learn in the labs, so I think that will be the next step."

Then I ask Tanya about costs. The process is funded by life insurance policies, although cash prepayment is also an option. At the time of my visit, it cost $50,000 for neuropreservation and $120,000 for whole-body suspension. Some of that money pays for the preserving process. The rest goes into a trust fund that provides for long-term storage and maintenance.

"We will need money to revive them," Tanya says, "and then we will need money to send them to school and/or to begin the reeducation process that will have to occur. The revival scenarios are just too speculative right now," she concedes.

We follow Tanya from the operating room to the "patient care bay," where the actual bodies and heads are. I half expect to see a bunch of giant fish tanks, with bodies and heads trapped in big blocks of ice. The reality is a bit anticlimactic, but at least I won't embarrass myself by fainting in front of the others. It's a big room with twenty-four-foot ceilings. There's a low, distinctive hum of electricity. Against one wall a row of large stainless steel tanks, called dewars, stand at attention. The bodies and heads are inside. (The word *dewar* comes from Sir James Dewar, of scotch-producing fame, who invented the first vacuum bottles in the 1800s. A Dewar's on ice would be nice right about now.) Tanya explains that each dewar can hold up to four bodies and five heads. Each head is placed in a huge pot that looks like any other large pot in anyone's kitchen.

The room is immaculate, anonymous, soothing. You can easily forget that human remains are floating inside those stainless steel containers. I thought the room would smell of alcohol or something, but the only thing I can smell is my Tiffany perfume.

Alcor moved to the Arizona desert from its original site outside Los Angeles in the early 1990s, to get out of the earthquake zone. After all, it wouldn't do their patients much good to be decanted by a major trembler. Tanya claims that the Scottsdale facility is totally safe and secure. The dewars are virtually indestructible, and the room has fail-safe backup against power outages.

"We can keep someone in these tanks for literally millions of years without deterioration," she says.

I'm surprised to hear the demographics of Alcor's client list. I expected it to be all wealthy, older white men, with the budgets to afford this highly speculative option, and the equally large egos to seek it out. Tanya claims most members are currently young and healthy. "We have highly educated people. We have a much higher demographic of Ph.D.'s and M.D.'s than typical demos would indicate. We are growing on the family scale." She says there are now members on every continent but Antarctica.

I turn to Jack and ask him if he believes in the hereafter.

"Of course I do!" he professes. "This is not against God's plan. He is allowing us to live longer and longer, so why not live two hundred years or a thousand years or as long as the universe lasts? And then when that comes to an end, I will go on to heaven."

Tanya is impressively sanguine about the gamble that Alcor represents. "It's either going to work or it's not," she says with a shrug, leading us out through steel doors. "That's what it boils down to."

When the others have left, Tanya leads me down a hallway to the office of Alcor's CEO, Joseph Waynick. He turns out to be a Denzel Washington look-alike with a warm handshake. He asks me if I have time to do him a favor. It seems there was a problem with a previous photo shoot for Alcor's information materials, and they need a model for the reshoot. Would I be willing . . . ?

I'm handed a work shirt and gloves, placed behind a CPR mannequin, and the photo shoot commences. As it proceeds, I ask Waynick some routine questions. The answers I get are anything but the expected, as I quickly discover he's a man solidly tethered to reality.

Born in New Jersey, Waynick joined the Marine Corps, and later was an executive with American Express. He retired at forty-one and started a graphic design company. He was a member of Alcor when, at the end of 2003, the presiding CEO was diagnosed with cancer and he was asked to step in.

I expect to hear "atheist" when I ask him about his beliefs. Instead, I hear something I never would have guessed: Waynick is an elder in his Seventh-day Adventist church. There is a sharpness and depth when he discusses his beliefs; something comes alive behind his eyes.

"As it says in Ecclesiastes, the dead know nothing," he declares. He believes that you can't go to heaven until Jesus returns, so until then, the dead are in a sleeping state. He feels he's merely prolonging his life by using cryogenics. "I'm going to heaven when I die. I want to use cryogenics to see how long I can live."

The bottom line is a matter of philosophy. Similar to the ongoing debate over whether life begins at conception or birth, Alcor members ask when is a person dead, when the brain ceases to function or when the heart stops? As far as they're concerned, the answer's obvious: No one is dead as long as the brain has a chance to live.

No one I speak to at Alcor seems to be trying to "cheat death." None of them thinks he or she can be immortal. They just want to prolong their life. They think of themselves as time travelers or explorers. I wonder if people thought Christopher Columbus had lost his mind because he wanted to see what lay beyond his comfortable world. Alcor members are daring to dream, to wonder what lies outside what society thinks is real or normal. Like Columbus, they're attempting an incredible voyage.

And we all know what happened to Columbus—he returned.

Romeo and Juliet

We all know that "a pair of star-crossed lovers take their lives" in William Shakespeare's *Romeo and Juliet*. But nothing prepares us for the spectacle of watching them do so in director Baz Luhrmann's innovative and stunning 1996 film version, set in a contemporary alternate universe, not unlike Southern California. Upon hearing of Juliet Capulet's (Claire Danes) death, Romeo Montague (Leonardo DiCaprio) breaks into the family chapel and then, as huge neon-blue crosses show the way, he takes a symbolic trip down the flower-strewn aisle to find Juliet's bier, surrounded by tiers of two thousand candles. Lying in her funeral bed, wearing her wedding dress, she represents his beginning and his end.

Imitation of Life

In the hands of melodrama master Douglas Sirk, the funeral
scene in *Imitation of Life* (a 1959 remake of John M. Stahl's
1934 version, both based on the Fannie Hurst book) became
one of the biggest tearjerkers in film history. Annie Johnson
(Juanita Moore) tells her lifelong friend Lora Meredith (Lana
Turner), a woman to whom Annie has acted as a housemaid all
those years, that she believes our wedding day and the day we
die are the great events of our life. "I want to go the way I
planned. No mourning, but proud and high-stepping like I was
going to glory," she says, and Sirk doesn't spare any detail. As
light filters through the brilliant stained-glass cathedral win-
dows, and multihued floral arrangements bank a white casket
covered with a blanket of snowy flowers, Mahalia Jackson sings
"Trouble of the World" from the pulpit. Then, as a New
Orleans–style band leads the way, Annie's casket is displayed in
a glass hearse carriage, pulled by four white horses, while her
commingled communities—black and white—line the streets
to pay their respects. Making a cameo in the crowd is Hattie
McDaniel, who played Mammy in another Technicolor epic,
Gone With the Wind.

✳

CHAPTER EIGHT

◎

Ashes to Ashes, Dust to Jewelry

I have a problem. My friends call it a fantastic habit; my husband calls it an expensive addiction. I love to shop for, buy, and wear jewelry. Not every day, mind you, maybe not every week, but at least once a month I have to venture out for what I call jewelry retail therapy. My purchases have two things in common: big pieces, always unique.

In the mid–nineteenth century, Queen Victoria had the same "problem." When Prince Albert died in 1861, this gal after my own heart broke tradition by making up a new tradition. Queen Victoria, widowed at forty-two, issued a mandate that only mourning jewelry, which included jewelry made of the deceased's hair, could be worn. She proceeded to wear mourning dress and mourning jewelry and accessories for the next forty years, creating one of the biggest fashion trends England has ever seen. The hair of a deceased loved one or friend was made into jewelry items that functioned as keepsakes, as mementos and reminders that they were never far away.

More than one hundred years later, Queen Victoria's fashion trend has reappeared in an unlikely place—Janesville, Wisconsin. For more than twelve years, Joni Cullen and Lisa Saxer-Buros of the Madelyn Company have been making keepsake pendants made of deceased loved ones' hair. Madelyn Company can incorporate dried flowers, cremated remains, or soil from the gravesite into the pendants, which can be worn or displayed in a glass dome.

It started in March 1992, when Lisa's mother, Madelyn Saxer, died. Lisa and Joni, friends since the seventh grade, went out to dinner with their husbands. Lisa showed Joni a piece of jewelry she had made that had strands of her mother's hair. Over the course of dinner the couples discussed what a great idea this would be, "to enable others to cope more easily, to hold a source of comfort in their hands and to find peace in their hearts," Joni explains.

So Madelyn Company was born. The two Wisconsin housewives and mothers got busy. "The first thing we did was go to a local hairdresser to ask if they had ever seen anything on the market like this, and we found out they hadn't," Joni recalls. "We went to our first funeral convention about ten years ago with just a couple of pieces. "

The "couple of pieces" they started out with have grown into more than seventy different designs for pendants, including sterling silver crosses; laser-engraved photos; quartz crystals; gold, silver, or pewter hearts; and a nature collection featuring butterflies, roses, turtles, doves, maple leaves, and acorns of brass. They also offer ornate, antique silver-and-glass cylinders I bet Queen Victoria would have loved.

Prices range from $1,000 to as little as $60. "We wanted everyone who's grieving to be able to afford one of our pendants," Joni tells me.

The process begins with the funeral director or distributor showing the family the presentation case or brochure with all the different keepsake pendants in it. When the family selects a pendant, the funeral director fills it and seals it right there. "We just don't want to take the chance of anything being lost by sending it to us," Joni explains. "Engraving takes a week or two, but everything else can be done in about a day."

Madelyn Company is a wholesaler to the funeral industry. "The consumer cannot purchase directly from us, but they can go to our Web site and call for a catalog," Joni says. "Or we can help them find a funeral director or distributor."

"All the new things happening in the funeral industry now have evolved from a personal story," Joni has discovered. "And Madelyn Company is no different."

"My mother's view on life was inspirational," Lisa says of the company's namesake. "She used to say, 'Love the moment,' and 'Death is the greatest adventure of all.'"

I love that on my way to that adventure, I can still shop.

CHAPTER NINE

○

Going Out with a Bang

"Had a blast!" are not words you would usually use to describe a funeral. But these exact words are uttered over and over when folks recall the funeral of Opal Alice Drobnis.

This may be because Opal was packed into large firework shells, which were placed on a barge named *Heaven Sent,* which was towed out from Los Angeles's Marina del Rey by a boat named *Shot in the Dark,* while her family followed on a sailboat named *Silver Eagle.* This caravan proceeded three miles out to sea toward a glorious sunset that gradually faded into a clear night with a full moon.

When they reached their destination, the captain of the *Silver Eagle* orated. "We have gathered on these beautiful waters of the Pacific Ocean to do honor and praise to the life and memory of Opal Alice Drobnis. We have gathered here in celebration of death, and in so doing, in celebration of life. We will now scatter the ashes. Fire away."

And as the song "Angels Among Us" played, Opal shot up from the barge and exploded in fountains and starbursts of fireworks. For a full five minutes she spread herself in brilliant colors and gay patterns against the moonlit sky, and her cremains gently drifted down to scatter on the dark water.

Everyone on board agreed that it didn't feel like a funeral at all. It was a celebration. And at prices that start at $3,500, it costs a lot less than most traditional funeral arrangements, too.

Opal's son Nick Drobnis is president of Angels Flight Fireworks. He laughs when I ask how the company began.

"My partner, Jeff Marsh, and I were working at a local theme park, in charge of the fireworks. Surrounded by all those explosives, we began to think about our own mortality." They got to talking about how they wanted to be memorialized when they died, and that's when Nick said he'd like his ashes to be packed into fireworks and shot into the air.

It wasn't until fifteen years later, when the two began to attend funerals of friends and family, that they decided to put Nick's idea into action. That was in 1990, but it took several years to obtain all the permits and licenses required from all the pertinent regulatory agencies.

"We had to deal with the Coast Guard, and the FAA, and the fire department, and the ATF, and the cemetery board," Nick recalls. Angels Flight's first service was for a ten-year-old boy whose parents were divorced. Nick sadly tells the story. "They were sharing custody. The little boy was with his dad and began to complain of a stomachache. So the father took him to the doctor, who said he had the flu. He brought the boy back to the mom's house and the boy kept complaining of a stomachache, so they took him to the emergency room." There he was told he had the flu. The boy went to sleep that night and didn't wake up.

The distraught mother told Nick that she couldn't bear putting her vibrant little boy into the ground. After the service, she said to him, "This is the first time since this whole thing started that I have felt at peace." Nick knew at that moment that he was in the right business.

Today, Nick says, "Our customers come from all over the nation. We're doing one or two services a month now."

Services are tailored for each client. For instance, UCLA alumni have been shot off in blue and gold fireworks. Some clients prefer to have the service on the beach rather than the boat. It's more economical for a larger family, "because they can avoid the cost of a larger boat," explains Nick. (The *Silver Eagle* can accommodate only six people, though Nick has arranged for boats that can carry as many as 120.) "Other families like the beach because they just don't want to get on a boat, or they want the freedom to do more things."

Angels Flight requires two weeks to pull all the permits and organize the service. "If the family lives within a fifty-mile radius, we'll pick up the remains. If not, we ask that they give us the remains one full day in advance," Nick says. The cremains are packed into ten large fireworks shells. These are shot off with one hundred others to make a full display.

Nick says that families will often come back to the beach or to charter a boat on the anniversary of the service.

"Whatever you do with your loved one," Nick tells me, "it's the final image of them that you hold in your mind for the rest of your life. Whether it's a regular funeral or a scattering, that's what you'll remember. I offer fireworks. What's better than that?"

ELOQUENT EULOGIES

Jack Benny (1894–1974)

"He was stingy to the end. He gave us only eighty years, and it wasn't enough."

—Bob Hope

George Burns (1896–1996)

"As he often said, he knew entrances and exits. And last Saturday, he knew it was time to go."

—movie executive Irving Fein

Screenwriter Dalton Trumbo (1905–1976)

"At rare intervals, there appears among us a person whose vir-
tues are so manifest to all . . . who lives his whole life in such
harmony with the surrounding community that he is revered
and loved by everyone with whom he comes in contact. Such
a man Dalton Trumbo was not."

—fellow writer Ring Lardner

Bette Davis (1908–1989)

"Hang on to your seats. It's going to be a bumpy eternity."

—James Woods

Robert Taylor (1911–1969)

"Millions who only knew him by way of the silver screen . . .
remember with gratitude that in the darkened theater he
never embarrassed them in front of the children."

—Ronald Reagan

Mickey Mantle (1931–1995)

"You know, it occurs to me as we're all sitting here thinking of
Mickey, he's probably somewhere getting an earful from
Casey Stengel, and no doubt quite confused by now."

—Bob Costas

CHAPTER TEN

◎

Close Encounter of Another Kind

In my part of the world, in the farthest left corner of Texas, where it and Mexico and New Mexico all meet, we have plenty of opportunities to go out to a ranch on a dark night and look up at the stars. On one of these dark, star-filled, moonless nights, if you *don't* see a UFO, you've either been drinking too many cervezas, or you're not looking up, or both.

So when I decided to go meet a man who claims to see blue, hairless aliens, and makes his own wine, and mummifies people and animals . . . heck, I felt like I was going to visit a relative. A relative who literally lives on the wrong side of the tracks.

To get to his house, you drive over some railroad tracks into a neighborhood of junkyards and warehouses. Turn left at the huge silver silo, and you can't miss it. Actually, you won't see his house at first. That's hidden behind the two-story pyramid in his front yard. In bright sunlight, the anodized copper that sheaths the pyramid gleams like gold. The square base is forty feet to a side; the peak is twenty-six feet high. It would stand out in any neighborhood, let alone against this drab industrial backdrop of cinder-block sheds and rusty machinery.

A wrought-iron fence in a colorful grapevine pattern surrounds the property, adding a disconcertingly homey touch. Near the pyramid there's a ranch-style entrance gate, with one word on it in big gold letters: SUMMUM—as in *summum bonum*, Latin for the highest good, the peak of human potential.

I'm standing there gazing up at the pyramid glistening against a bright blue sky when the man who built it comes bustling out of the small house nearby. Corky Ra is a fit, medium-built sixty-year-old who looks fifty. He has sparkling blue eyes, and though his hair has thinned on top, a blondish-gray ponytail hangs to the middle of his back. In jeans and a flannel shirt, he reminded me of a younger Willie Nelson—same calm mannerisms, same kind smile, same aging-hippie look.

Corky is the founder of Summum, a philosophy (or what the IRS refers to as a church) that incorporates mummification, winemaking, and a close encounter of another kind: sexual ecstasy. He claims to have a global following of more than 250,000 people. It's all centered on this pyramid in his front yard, in the most unlikely city in the world for this kind of activity: Salt Lake City, Utah, the heart of Mormon country.

Where he's on the wrong side of the tracks in more ways than one.

Corky pushes a button and a door in one side of the pyramid cantilevers open like something out of a sci-fi movie. It even makes a sound like the elevator doors on Captain Kirk's *Enterprise.* I feel like I'm stepping into the mother ship. Inside, the four triangular walls soar up in perfect proportions to the peak high above my head. Near the peak, three walls bear beautiful painted murals. One has a sort of sci-fi theme. Another features Egyptian-looking figures, and the inscription:

> Creation manifests when balance is perfected between the opposites. By applying higher law against lower laws, the creation becomes divine.

> —Summum

Under that mural is a large altar. A six-foot mummy stands at either end. The one on the right is entirely wrapped in white gauze, with its hands folded across its chest. The other stands inside an ornate casket of gold that looks like something out of the King Tut exhibit. The altar is set with a red tablecloth and bouquets of pretty flowers. Fist-sized crystals of clear quartz line the altar, which is also adorned with nine slim white candles and four wine goblets.

But what really catches my eye are the cats standing below the altar. Three of them, in a perfect line, standing completely still, as though on guard. The two at the end are shiny black, the one in the middle, golden. They're still as statues. Well, they *are* statues—with mummified house cats inside. Corky tells me their names are Oscar, Vincent, and Smokey. Elsewhere in the pyramid, a few others stand mute and regal. Corky is very fond of cats (as were the ancient Egyptians), and looks after a number of neighborhood strays. And when they pass on, he pays them the ultimate compliment of mummifying them and encasing them in these beautiful bronze statuettes (technically referred to as "mummiforms").

Even more impressive—downright alarming, at first glance—are the two mummified dogs who stand just inside the doorway. There's Butch, a Doberman entirely encased in glistening gold, and a brawny mastiff who's just begun to get his golden coating over his gauze wrappings. Smaller, more humbly wrapped mummies of a parrot, a parakeet, and a peacock lie strewn at Butch's feet like forgotten chew toys.

More Egyptian-themed objects are gathered under the altar. Two small pyramids, three golden statuettes of Egyptian male gods with a certain part of their anatomy very prominent, and last but certainly not least, a gigantic (but does size really matter?) golden phallus. You get the feeling that the women of ancient Egypt must have been a happy and satisfied bunch.

Besides the altar, the pyramid is furnished with large, comfortable couches that face each other across a plush carpet. Most likely, the carpet was installed not only for comfort but to keep the sound down when Corky broadcasts his Thursday-night meditation and philosophy instruction programs on Internet TV. The camera and a small computer station stand on one side of the room.

Corky and I sit facing each other on those couches, and he explains how all this came to be. On November 3, 1975, Corky, still going by his birth name, Claude Rex Norwell, was a successful young businessman. Born and raised in Salt Lake City, he was the son of a prosperous contractor and a member of the Mormon faith—the Church of the Latter Day Saints, or LDS. Recently divorced from the mother of his two children, he was working as an administrative manager for a large graphics supply company.

A pretty ordinary life—until that night in 1975, when he came home (back then he lived in the upscale Mount Olympus neighborhood, at the foot of the mighty Wasatch Mountains, which provide a spectacular background for the city) and went down to his newly constructed den to relax. That's when he began to see aliens.

Corky has told the alien story to reporters and other visitors so often since then that he's sick of talking about it. Instead, he hands me a brochure that he wrote explaining it. Basically, it's the same old alien-encounter story—your body transported into another dimension, you walk through glass, you telepathically communicate with blue hairless aliens who download certain information and processes into your brain. You change your name to Summum Bonum Amon (aka "Corky") Ra, start a religion, begin to mummify people and ferment wine . . . blah blah blah, same ole, same ole, boring.

After a decade of visits from the extraterrestrial Blue Man Group, Corky founded Summum in 1985 to begin practicing and teaching what they'd shown him. Not surprisingly, there's a lot of it that echoes ancient Egyptian beliefs and practices, with a strong added element of Buddhist meditation, references to the *Tibetan Book of the Dead,* and the Hindu practice of Tantric sex.

Mummification is central to the practices of the group. Although we associate mummies with Egypt, the practice was once common around the world, from Chile to China, from Alaska to Australia. The early Christians practiced it; most of the popes' earthly remains have been preserved through mummification. Today, though, it's quite rare—in fact, Summum claims to be the only group in the world offering the service.

Corky, who is a licensed funeral director in the state of California (where, I wasn't amazed to learn, Summum has many adherents), explained the process to me.

"The body is transported to a funeral home, where it is prepared for traditional viewing and services. After the services, surgeons called nanogeneticists begin the mummification process. The body is bathed and cleaned, and an incision is made to remove the internal organs—everything but the brain. The organs are thoroughly cleansed and placed back into the body. The incision is left open so that the organs can receive further treatment. The body is immersed in a special preservation solution made up of certain liquids, some of which are chemicals used in genetic engineering. The body remains submerged for six months, long enough to achieve maximum penetration of the fluids. The body is removed from the immersion tank, cleansed again, and then covered with a lotion. Several layers of gauze are wrapped around the body. A polyurethane membrane is applied over the gauze, forming a permanent seal. Then follows a layer of fiberglass and resin. The body is encased in a bronze or stainless steel mummiform. The mummiform is filled with an amber resin, completely surrounding the mummy and protecting the perfection that has been created. Finally, the openings in the mummiform are welded closed. The process takes about a year."

You might think that a process that can preserve the body for thousands of years is all about the physical—a way of "cheating death," like cryogenics. But as Corky and his colleagues explain it to me, in fact, for them the focus is really a spiritual one.

"Mummification is much more than just the body," Corky says confidently. Mummification is only the first step in what Summum offers; the second, and apparently more important aspect, is what Summum calls "transference." For Summum, the mummified body is like a spiritual tool, and serves as a reference point for the soul after death, preventing what might be considered "postmortem panic." Summum offers appropriate ceremonies to help the spirit make the transition to its next destination in a guided, awakened manner. Think of it as a roadmap for the spirit, one that points out the dangers and tourist traps to avoid.

Bernie Aua is a forty-seven-year-old Web master and Internet specialist who maintains the Summum Web site. He also was born and raised in Salt Lake City, but grew up Roman Catholic. He has been a member of Summum since 1977. I asked him why he chose to be mummified when he dies.

"Mummification is a guide to whatever your next life might be, and that's my main reason for doing this—to make the most of the transition," he replied. "The spirit is eternal. I don't have a fear of death like I used to. I have a totally different appreciation of death now, and of mummification's being a journey in that transition. I will end up in the new existence that will continue on."

"The concept has been around for thousands of years," Corky tells me. The Egyptians believed that the body was a manifest form of the soul, a reflection of a divine inner being, a perfectly integrated, orchestrated union of entity and vehicle. Even after death, an ethereal bond between the soul and body remained. Preserving the body or the identity of the person was the most critical thing to do in order for the person's soul to reach its destination in the afterlife. The entire culture of the ancient Egyptians was based on their belief in the afterlife, and they spent their lives preparing for it. The pharaohs built their elaborate tombs for their mummified bodies, and stocked them with all the things they might need in the next life, including money, slaves, and wives. But common people also tried to equip themselves for the journey, and often spent a large amount of what they earned on the preparations.

"After we go out on a trip, we always come home," Bernie Aua explains. "Well, our bodies are a home, too." He means a home for the soul. "I want my preserved body to last a long time," he says, so that no matter how long his soul may wander in the afterlife, it will have a home to return to.

Corky explained that you don't have to be a Summum member to be mummified; they can do the mummifying and ritual of transference according to whatever religion you believe in. (Unless you belong to a religion that forbids mummification, of course.) When I met him he said that over one thousand people had signed up to be mummified; probably the most famous, according to an article linked to Summum's Web site, was Mohamed Al Fayed, father of Dodi, who died with Princess Di in that horrible car crash.

It's not cheap. At the time of our meeting, the costs of mummification for a human started at $67,000; dogs started at $27,000 and cats at $6,000. (Told you Corky has a soft spot for them.) "Some people want a Ferrari, some people don't," Corky said with a shrug. "We're like a Ferrari dealership—the high end." Then again, he recommends that you purchase a universal life insurance policy (pre-need) to cover the costs.

When I visited, Corky was getting ready to build a new underground mausoleum right on the property, so that members who wished to could have their mummies housed right there, next to the pyramid. He explained that they can do that because of "an old Utah law, one that was written when Utah was a territory, stating you can bury a person on church ground." A similarly old law allows Summum to bottle its own wine in the notoriously dry state of Utah—but only if it's used for religious purposes. (I'm not sure which old law allows for the group's espousal of Tantric sexual practices, but that's a subject for another book.)

Even though mummification might seem odd by today's standards, Summum brings back the ancient tradition with a modern twist. They remind us of the concept of an afterlife, so that we can try to remember that we aren't simply composed of bones and blood. That we are human beings with the capacity to think, to feel, to love, and to understand that behind our eyes there is something else to each of us, an essence that makes each of us unique. Summum believes that uniqueness lives on after our bodies give out. That essence is our soul, dimensionless and eternal.

Maybe if we knew our own spirit we would understand

that we don't ever die, really; we still maintain our personalities, our dreams, our desires, our feelings.

"You remain capable of feelings and are very much aware of incidents taking place," Summum member Ron Temu, also a licensed funeral director, said to me. "Your attention remains intact."

As I was leaving, Corky graciously gave me some Summum literature—as well as a bottle of that sacramental wine—and a compliment.

"You look just like my daughter," he said, grinning. "Older version, but just like her."

Hey, maybe I did visit a relative.

CHAPTER ELEVEN

◎

When a Diamond Really *Is* Your Best Friend

I buy a new diamond wedding ring every year.

Think about that for a moment—and, if you are so inclined, maybe say a little prayer on my husband's behalf. Yes, I have been married over six years, and I still buy wedding magazines to riffle through the diamond ring ads, hoping that one day I'll find the perfect one, the ring I can look at every day for the rest of my life and be satisfied.

So I know why I like the idea behind LifeGem, a company that creates high-quality diamonds by compressing carbon, the primary element of all diamonds, at pressures that re-create those that produce diamonds deep inside the Earth.

Man-made diamonds are nothing new, of course. The twist here is that the carbon LifeGem uses happens to come from cremains. Prices range from $2,500 to $14,000.

I ask Greg Herro, the CEO of LifeGem, what I suppose is an obvious question: How does a guy who graduated summa cum laude from Illinois State University with degrees in industrial technology and graphic communication end up turning dead people into diamonds? What was his motivation?

"The overwhelming desire to do something phenomenal to change the way people look at death," he promptly replies, revealing a thick Chicago accent. "It is not in my personality to want to do normal, humdrum things."

Greg is a man in his late thirties who looks like he'd be more comfortable on Wall Street than in Elk Grove Village, Illinois. "I don't have a jewelry background or a funeral background," he goes on. "But what I do have for a background is the unwillingness to let things stop. This is something I felt so strongly about and couldn't imagine not being able to accomplish."

Greg conceived of LifeGem in 1999 and incorporated in 2001. "Initially, we had four partners who were willing to help offer the product in Illinois. Now we have over two thousand partners here and in the UK, Japan, Canada, Australia, South Africa, the Netherlands, Belgium, and Hungary."

Of course I'm not alone in my love of diamonds. The company has gotten great publicity, from BBC World News to National Public Radio.

Greg says clients contact the company through its Web site, or through their funeral director. He categorizes them according to need.

"There are three types of need," he explains. "Pre-need, when people are looking at this and saying, this is what I want for my future. Then there's at-need, when you've just lost a loved one. And post-need, when you lost someone a long time ago and finally have made a decision on what you want to do."

Luckily, the process works no matter how long you've had the ashes. LifeGem can also make a diamond out of your pet.

I tell Greg that I'd like to turn some of my husband's ashes into a diamond. When he offers his condolences, I explain that Barry is not only alive but the picture of health in his mid-forties. I'm just planning ahead. But I have a problem. According to their information, the largest diamond LifeGem makes is one carat. I tell Greg that just won't be large enough.

"We are working on bigger diamonds," he tells me, "but it's hard to do. The longer the diamond is in the press, the more the surface area is expanding from a little speck to where it ends. And the more surface area you have, the more chance for unacceptable inclusions." Meaning flaws. "It's a matter of balance."

I decide that if my husband dies first I'm going to make him into a one-carat diamond bracelet link. And if I change my mind later, that's also okay—Greg tells me he can make up to fifty diamonds from a single person's ashes.

LifeGem diamonds come in three cuts—round, princess, and radiant. And it recently introduced yellow diamonds, in a gradation of intensities Greg compares to the different hues of a sunset. The company prefers to set your diamond for you in custom-designed jewelry rather than send it to you loose. I get the sense Greg doesn't like the idea of your loved one just sitting on your dresser.

The process starts with your separating about eight ounces of your loved one's (or pet's) ashes and shipping them in a secure plastic bag or container. Cremated remains cannot be sent back, so LifeGem encourages you not to send all of the remains.

Creating the diamond takes about six months—not bad, considering it takes Mother Nature one to three million years to do the same. Carbon is extracted from the cremains, then heated to extremely high temperatures, under special conditions, which converts the carbon to graphite. The graphite is then placed in one of LifeGem's diamond presses, replicating the forces of nature. The longer it's in the press, the larger the rough diamond crystal that's produced. Finally, diamond-cutters facet the gem according to your specifications.

All LifeGem diamonds come with a lifetime guarantee against any defects. The diamonds are inspected, graded, and certified by gemologists trained at the Gemological Institute of America, who attest to its cut, color, clarity, and carat weight.

Greg tells me that people react in funny ways when they get their loved ones back as precious jewels. "This is the most amazing part of what we do, and it's why we do what we do. People never react the way they expected to. They think they're getting a diamond and that's where it ends, but when they actually hold it in their hands, it's emotionally overwhelming and joyful and sad and everything wrapped up into one. One thing we did not anticipate is their having *fun* with their Life-Gem diamond."

He tells me of one swinging couple "who went to the same Friday-night hangout spot every week with their friends." When the husband died, his widow had a LifeGem diamond made from his ashes. "Then she had her wedding rings melted down into a cross, and put the LifeGem in the center of it. She wears it on a necklace. Every Friday night she still meets their friends at the hangout, and they always ask her if she brought her husband. They buy him a beer, and she takes off her cross and dips it in the beer."

Sounds like my kind of crowd. Later, I tell my husband that I'm going to turn him into a diamond and dip him in a shot of tequila once a week.

He gives me a funny look, but I'm used to that.

OUT OF THE BOX
AND AHEAD OF THEIR TIME

There was no way the life of Hunter S. Thompson could ever end without a bang. So it's no surprise that the legendary journalist and hotel marauder specified that after he died he wanted his ashes shot out of a cannon. "He loved explosions," said his wife, Anita, who complied with this request. In August 2005, Thompson's ashes were propelled from a cannon mounted inside a fifty-three-foot-high sculpture of the journalist's trademark "gonzo fist."

But Thompson isn't the only rugged individualist who was an out-of-the-box thinker about his own death. Civil rights champion and defense attorney Clarence Darrow, known for defending John T. Scopes from the charge of violating the Tennessee antievolution law by teaching Darwin's theory, was a freethinking agnostic. In support of his belief that the earth is the home and the only home of man, Darrow's ashes were scattered from a bridge in Chicago's 1,055-acre Jackson Park. Because he promised to return to Chicago at ten A.M. each March 13—the anniversary of his death—every year on that date people gather to wait on the "Darrow" Bridge.

Although writer Richard Wright would publish many works, he is best remembered for *Black Boy,* a memoir of his painful upbringing and his family's devastating persecution by the KKK. When longtime expatriate Wright died in Paris on November 28, 1960, his final request only underscored the book's significance: just as he wished, his ashes were mixed with the ashes of a copy of his autobiographical masterpiece.

Folksinger and Chicago native Steve Goodman was a rabid baseball fan who so loved his hometown Cubs that he wrote a song called "A Dying Cub Fan's Last Request." The lyrical appeal to "Build a big fire on home plate out of your Louisville Sluggers baseball bats, and toss my coffin in" was honored when a portion of his remains was buried beneath home plate at Wrigley Field. Goodman, who died on September 20, 1984, would have been thrilled to know that four days later, the Cubs won the pennant.

Flying Burrito Brother Gram Parsons, credited with "inventing" country rock, made a pact with his road manager, Phil Kaufman, that the survivor would spread the other's ashes over Cap Rock at Joshua Tree in the Mohave/Sonoran Desert. But in 1973, when Parsons died from a drug overdose, the musician's family made other arrangements for a burial in New Orleans. So Kaufman and a friend stole Parsons's body from Los Angeles airport and drove to Joshua Tree, where they poured gasoline into the coffin and set it on fire. The men were arrested several days later, but since there was no law against stealing a body, they paid only a $700 fine for burning the coffin.

CHAPTER TWELVE

◎

The Final Frontier

You don't need millions of dollars to go into space anymore. For as little as $995, you can boldly go where no man has gone before.

The only thing is, you have to be dead and cremated. Then Charlie Chafer's company, Space Services Inc., will pack your ashes into a rocket and shoot them into space.

Charlie was sixteen years old on July 20, 1969, when man first walked on the moon. "I grew up as a child of Mercury, Gemini, and Apollo," he says in a slow drawl. "I guess, like any kid, I wanted to be an astronaut. But I'm six-two, and well, that just wasn't going to work."

Charlie studied for a career in foreign service at Georgetown University in Washington. Little did he know his career would be in a foreign service of quite a different kind.

"I got reintroduced to space in the mid-seventies, while a student at Georgetown, when I read a Sunday editorial from a Princeton professor named Gerard O'Neill. He had a concept of moving humanity off this planet—the ultimate environmental program. That caught my attention."

The article rekindled Charlie's interest in space activity. In graduate school he wrote a book for NASA on the social-science implications of space exploration.

Years later, Charlie met a Houston man named David Hannah, who had made a fortune in real estate—and, more important, had read the same article that Charlie did. In quint-essential Texas style, Hannah had started his own space company and was building a private launch vehicle.

"I was fortunate to meet him and catch the fever," Charlie recalls, "and he needed someone in D.C. to help develop and market the idea of private space flights." The head of the team was former Mercury and Apollo astronaut Deke Slayton. In 1982, the three of them launched the first privately funded vehicle ever sent into outer space.

In 1984, a company in Florida called the Celestis Group approached Slayton with the idea of launching cremated remains into space. Charlie's job was to obtain the required permission from the federal government. "Some of the very earliest regulatory permissions the government gave the private sector to conduct space missions was for launching cremated remains," he explains.

It wasn't until 1997 that Celestis Inc.—a descendant of the Celestis Group, formed by Charlie and a partner—had its first successful memorial launch. The payload included the cremains of a broad spectrum of people, including Gene Roddenberry, the creator of *Star Trek;* Dr. Timothy Leary, known for his inner-space explorations; and Gerard O'Neill, the Princeton professor who'd reignited Charlie's passion for space.

Celestis would complete four more such missions, sending the ashes of some 250 people into space. In 1999, at NASA's request, the company sent the cremains of legendary space scientist Dr. Eugene Shoemaker to the moon. The package crashed into the lunar south pole, making Dr. Shoemaker the first man ever to be buried on the moon.

In 2004, Celestis became part of a new company, Space Services Inc. SSI is preparing to launch the cremains of some 125 people, from all over the world and from all walks of life, into space. Of course, Charlie points out, to boost that many people into space, SSI can send only a small amount of each person's cremains, from one to seven grams. (Think of it as one to seven packets of sugar's worth.) These are sealed in a small canister that looks like a chrome lipstick holder, which is in turn attached to the spacecraft. Clients may request a small message or plaque, which have ranged from the *Star Trek*–themed "Live long and prosper," to "My God . . . It's full of stars!" from *2001: A Space Odyssey,* to more traditional notes such as "Dad, we love you."

SSI offers three different kinds of launches. You can have your ashes launched into earth orbit, for $995 to $5,300, depending on the number of grams. You can orbit or land on the moon ($12,500). And soon your cremains can be part of a Voyager mission into deep space ($12,500). The company hopes to launch two or three missions a year.

Many clients come to SSI through its Web site, and Charlie notes that funeral directors, mainly younger ones, have become interested in and excited about the program. "All the trends are pushing toward alternative arrangements," Charlie says. "We're at the beginning of a big growth curve. We now have over fifty funeral home partners all over the world."

Once a contract has been signed, SSI sends a kit to the family or funeral home, so that they can collect a "flight sample" of cremains and send them to SSI by certified U.S. mail. The sample is stored in a safe-deposit box in Houston until ninety days before the scheduled launch. At that point, the cremains are transferred into their flight container and transported to the launch vehicle.

As at NASA, launch dates sometimes have to be rescheduled, so the company posts updates on its Web site and contacts families. A memorial service is held the day before the launch. Families are briefed on the flight process, and allowed to get near the rocket. The next day, they're at the site when the rocket takes off.

"At the moment of the launch, when you're standing there watching it and you're personally connected to it in some way, it is an unbelievable feeling," Charlie says. "The power and the majesty of the rocket going off, and realizing that your loved one is achieving a lifelong dream of going into space . . . People scream and high-five each other."

When I was twelve years old, I sat in the backseat of my father's Lincoln Continental with one of my dad's good friends—astronaut Alan Shepard. It was a summer night and the moon was full. I glanced over and saw Shepard gazing up at the night sky.

"Admiral Shepard," I remember asking, "what do you think about when you see the moon?"

His voice was hushed when he replied, "Going to the moon was the zenith of my life. I can't wait to die and go back there."

Thanks to SSI, we can all go.

DEATH AND THE COMPUTER

Virtually Buried

We all know people who live on the Internet. Now you can die there, too.

The World Wide Cemetery (www.cemetery.org) is much like any conventional cemetery. It's open to the public. It's got monuments. But unlike the "real" ones, this virtual cemetery doesn't present upkeep costs or weather concerns. With some 30 million people around the globe currently accessing the Internet, friends, family, and people you have never met will be able to see you memorialized in moving images, sound, and photographs.

To get your monument into this virtual cemetery, you fill out a simple form. The fee for text is only fifteen dollars, and you can add additional files for only twenty dollars. A family page costs fifteen to forty dollars, depending on how many photos you want to include. And to let the deceased know that you've paid a visit, virtual flowers are available. Donations are requested.

*

Online Discount Casket Retailers

The Federal Trade Commission has legally barred mortuaries from refusing to use a casket purchased from an outside source. As a result, all sorts of opportunities are cropping up online for buying inexpensive or discount caskets, including:

www.funeralbiz.com—free shipping to most major metro areas

www.directcasket.com—next-day shipping all regions, $200 to $400

www.abettercasket.com—50 to 75 percent off retail prices

*

Netcast Funerals

EulogyCast (www.eulogycast.com) offers a secure, live broad-
cast of your funeral or memorial service to family and friends
around the world with Internet access. Similarly, Funeral-Cast
(www.funeral-cast.com) puts your loved one's funeral, memorial, and/or graveside service online, as well as death notices
and memorials.

✳

Online Obits

Legacy.com hosts the online obituary sites of more than 175
leading U.S. newspapers.

✳

Preplan Your Funeral

The Funeral Help Web site (www.funeral-help.com/software .html) offers software called "Going in Style" ($29.95) that helps you plan your last big event on earth.

CHAPTER THIRTEEN

※

We Are All Connected

I roll down my car window, crane my neck and listen to the aspen trees as our car begins the climb up to Ski Apache in Ruidoso, New Mexico. A breeze I can barely feel on my cheek will send the top of the tall aspen foliage into a whispering panic. My husband shares, as he has zillions of times, that aspen trees are the largest living organisms on the planet.

At the top of the mountain I stop and gaze down at the aspen groves. Hundreds of trees share the same root system, which in effect makes them all the same tree. Even what seems to be a dead tree may not be, because its roots, nurtured by the other trees, survive belowground. They are all connected.

You get the same feeling as you drive north from Spokane, Washington, past the resort town of Sandpoint, Idaho, to Celebration Forest. The tall spruce and pine seem to snap to attention as you approach; the maple and oak whisper to you as you pass.

Heidi Stockton is the president and director of marketing and sales of Celebration Forest. Her name fits her perfectly. She has hair so blond it's almost translucent, a sincere smile, and an inviting laugh. She's been president of the company since 1999.

Founder Dennis Clark was a professional forester for the state of Idaho. For many years friends and family would ask him to plant trees as memorials for their loved ones. He'd plant them on state park land, and the survivors would never know the exact location of "their" tree. Dennis wished there was a better way to plant memorial trees that folks could go visit, as they would a grave site. That's how he and his wife, Cherry, came up with the idea of planting a grove of their own, and created Celebration Forest in 1995.

Today Dennis does the planting and looks after the trees, while Heidi looks after the business. Celebration Forest is located in Bear Butte Grove, in the beautiful mountains of northern Idaho, just ten miles from Sandpoint and not far from the Canadian border. It's a wonderful area to visit, with snow-capped ski mountains and cold, crystal lakes, lush valleys rich with wildlife, and breathtaking vistas. Celebration Forest stays open year-round, including weekends and holidays, to make visiting easy.

The trees are planted in a grid; each one has a grid number, plus a laminated marker, making it easy for friends and family to find. You can also buy an engraved granite marker or granite bench and have it placed next to the tree.

You get to choose which of four types of trees to plant. The Christmasy spruces and fragrant pines are just two to three feet tall when planted, but they can grow to a towering one hundred feet. The maples' leaves flare from dark green in the summer to bright yellow or flaming red every autumn; some grow to be as tall as eighty feet. The oaks can also get that tall, spreading their gorgeous canopies overhead. All four types can live one hundred to two hundred years—a fitting memorial indeed. Celebration Grove is a permanent forest preserve, protected from harvesting and development.

How do people choose? Heidi tearfully recalls one client whose daughter was diagnosed with cancer in her early twenties. The mother "began looking into ways to memorialize her daughter, and she started talking to me about two years before her daughter passed away. I really got to know her. She called me the day her daughter died. She told me that her daughter was a bit eccentric, and she loved dyeing her hair different colors. The week before she passed away she dyed her hair red. So her mother bought a red maple tree."

The trees cost $79 to $149 each, and come with a two-year guarantee that Celebration Forest will replant any tree that does not take to the soil. But Heidi proudly points out that so far they've planted more than eight hundred trees, and they've "never had to replace one."

Heidi tells me that most clients find Celebration Forest on the Internet, but they also have a lot of word-of-mouth and repeat business. People purchase a tree for a friend or family member, she explains, "and 90 percent of our business is memorials."

A few people have had loved ones' cremated ashes scattered at the foot of their trees, Heidi says. "We dig up a row around the tree and scatter the cremated remains in it, then replace the earth. So the remains grow into the tree, and the tree becomes a part of a living legacy."

Heidi says that while Celebration Forest's clients come from all over the United States, most of them live in big cities, especially New York City and others in the Northeast, where an aerosol air freshener is as close as they get to the aroma of fresh pine. "They're not used to having forests in their backyards." Unlike visiting a traditional grave, coming to the memorial grove "makes them feel good. They can come back in a year or two, after they've gone through the initial grieving stage, to this fabulous resort town and visit their tree year-round. It's a happy remembrance."

Maybe life is just as simple as this. Maybe we're like the aspen groves, sharing the same basic design, all connected under the surface. When one of us dies, we rally around to nurture one another. We work together like that, just as nature does. And on some level we know that we never really die; we just pass beyond earthly perception and yet remain ourselves, kept alive through others' thoughts and in their memories.

IT'S YOUR FUNERAL

"Why buy a casket just for one day?" asks MHP Enterprises, a Canadian firm. Why not get years of use out of your casket while you're still living?

The company lets you reduce the burden of expensive funerals with unique alternatives: caskets that double as furniture until needed as your final resting place. MHP offers caskets as sofas ($2,995); casket coffee tables ($2,495); a casket entertainment center ($4,495); caskets as beds, phone booths, and bookcases; and even a casket billiard table. Custom orders are also welcome.

CHAPTER FOURTEEN

✺

Spirits in the Sky

Joanie and Clyde West were having a quiet family dinner at Clyde's brother's house in Florida in 1995 when the conversation turned to death. Clyde looked at his brother and announced that he and Joanie were going to be cremated. He then asked his brother to "put our butts in a balloon and send us off."

Joanie laughs, remembering the words that launched their new business.

"We owned a bridal shop and a balloon shop, and we put Teddy Bears in balloons for kids' parties," she continues in her calm Florida drawl. "So we thought it might be possible."

The next morning Joanie called her son George in New York City and asked his opinion. "George said to start with pets, so we did," Joanie remembers. The Florida couple applied for a patent, while George went to work on a business plan. Nearly two years later, the Eternal Ascent Society was patented and trademarked, and all the needed permits from the Coast Guard and FAA had been granted.

When I spoke to Joanie, Eternal Ascent had released more than one hundred high-altitude balloons, carrying the cremated remains of people from all over the country up, up, and away. The helium-filled balloons are five feet in diameter and in bright, cheery colors, making their ascent easy to track with the eye. On a clear day, Joanie says, you can track the balloon rising almost two miles, which generally takes about fifteen minutes. When it reaches an altitude of about five miles (26,000 feet or so), the balloon freezes (the temperature at that altitude is around forty degrees below zero), crystallizes, and shatters, scattering the ashes in the upper atmosphere.

Joanie says most people find Eternal Ascent through the Internet, then call to hear more about the services provided. Pricing starts at just under $1,000, with additional costs depending on how far Joanie and Clyde must travel. They'll go anywhere to perform the service, but they've also begun to franchise the operation, and hope someday to have franchisees in every state.

Ministers are always welcome at the launch. If children are attending, Joanie tells me, they are encouraged to write little notes to the departed on the surface of a smaller balloon, which is attached to the main one. "We use a rubber band to attach it—no ribbon and no strings. Everything is biodegradable. The balloons are one hundred percent latex." She explains that the ribbon and string, as well as the Mylar often used in other helium balloons, would not be environmentally sound to use, especially if they fell into the ocean, where they can endanger sea life.

"We had one gentleman, bless his heart, who was just devastated when his wife died," Joanie recalls. "He told me that now he talks to his wife every day by sending her a note on a balloon."

The process is quite simple. The balloon is filled with cremated remains, then inflated with the helium. Friends and family are encouraged to take hold of the balloon and release it together. Afterward, they receive a DVD recording and photos documenting the service.

Joanie's voice trembles as she tells me the story of Dawn, who was diagnosed with breast cancer at the age of thirty-three and did not inform her family until it was too late to save her. She died, leaving a bereaved husband and three young children, two sons and a daughter.

Dawn's ashes were launched in a balloon from the parking lot of their church, with more than 250 people in attendance. Her children wrote her little notes. One "was the cutest note I have ever seen," Joanie recalls. "It said, 'Mommy, I miss you and I am coming to see you.'"

Later, the husband called Joanie to tell her that the children were still crying for their mother. "I told him to go down to the store and get three balloons, blow them up, let the children write little notes on them, and release them." Now when the kids speak of their mom, they look up to the sky and point.

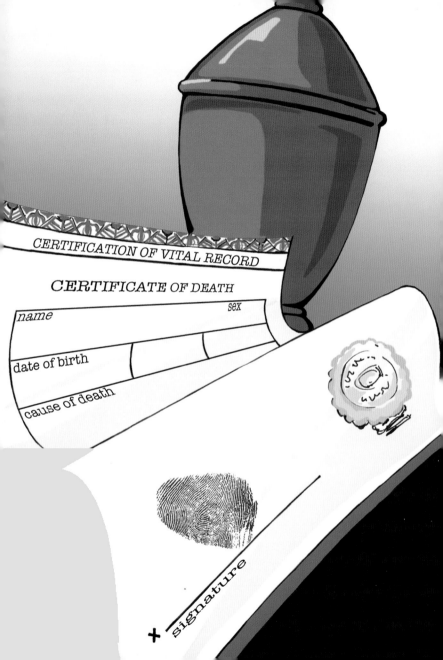

CHAPTER FIFTEEN

◎

Someday My Prints Will Come

I was the third of four children. Not lucky enough to be pampered like my little brother, Monte, the baby, or respected like my older brother, Mark. My sister, Jennifer, was the first girl, so that left me somewhere lost in the middle.

Somehow—and I still haven't quite figured this out—my fingerprints were always found in all the wrong places. Just mine, mind you, not anyone else's. I am still convinced that somehow, while I innocently and soundly slept at night, my horrible older sister, with nothing better to do than to make my life hell, sneaked into my room, covertly obtained my fingerprints, and then carefully put those indicting prints in all those wrong places. Like the newly polished dining room table, the freshly poured concrete outside all the new homes in our Austin neighborhood, and my father's waxed and spit-shined brown (always brown) Lincoln Continental.

But mostly in my mother's daily desserts. My mother, who must have taken a crash course with the FBI, never suspected any of my other siblings, or any visiting neighborhood kids, for that matter.

"Michelle, I see you've been in the chocolate cake again this morning!" she would screech from the kitchen.

"It wasn't me!" I would yell back.

"Yes, it was," my sister, daughter of Satan, would lob back. "Your fingerprints are in it."

"You are a stupid, fat liar," I'd counter.

But fingerprints don't lie.

In ancient Babylon, fingerprints were used as signatures in business transactions. Thumbprints have been found on clay seals from ancient China. A fourteenth-century Persian doctor, observing official government papers with fingerprints on them, noticed that no two were alike. Mark Twain used fingerprints as fictional devices in his *Life on the Mississippi* (1883) and *Pudd'n'head Wilson* (1894), in which fingerprints are evidence in a dramatic court trial.

Twain was writing around the time that British scientist Sir Francis Galton established a system for classifying the prints of all ten fingers, still the basis of modern fingerprinting. Fingerprinting would soon be used throughout the United States and Europe for identifying and convicting criminals. Today, the FBI claims to have more than 226 million fingerprints on file, representing 79 million people (mine included, thanks to my mother).

And since 1998, Thumbies Fingerprint Keepsakes "have been combining modern scanning technology with the ancient technique of lost wax casting" to create jewelry that preserves the unique prints of loved ones. You can have thumbprints, fingerprints, or infants' palm and footprints engraved as charms, bracelets, cuff links or tie tacks of sterling silver or gold. You can even wear your pets' paw or nose prints!

David Gordon founded Meadow Hill Company, Inc., aka Thumbies, when he "almost choked one night on a necklace his mother created out of his little girl's thumbprints," Adrienne Kalmes, director of sales, says, laughing. "He took that as a sign and started Thumbies."

Adrienne says that many people like to preserve the prints of their babies. "However, infants and children under the age of three pose a problem when it comes to capturing a reproducible print. While they have fingerprints, the defining ridges are too fine, so it's difficult to get a contrast. We recommend a hand- or footprint. Many hospitals today take hand- and footprints, so the parents may already have them. These can be scanned, and we can use that scan to make the pieces."

While individuals can purchase Thumbies through the company's Web site, Adrienne says about 85 percent of sales are through funeral homes, to families who want a unique keepsake of the departed loved one. "To have something to hold and touch that's a part of the person is something really special," she says.

Adrienne tells me of a man who knew he was going to die and decided to give his children and grandchildren Thumbies keepsakes. "At the funeral it was a surprise to all of them," she says. "When the funeral director handed them out to everyone, they were all taken aback and so grateful for his consideration."

Another touching Thumbies story concerns a man who died shortly before his daughter's wedding. The daughter wanted to call everything off, but the funeral director, who knew the family, told the daughter her father would want her to get married. Thumbies were made for everyone in the wedding party to wear in remembrance of him. After the wedding, the daughter thanked the funeral director and showed him on her bra strap where she had carefully placed her Thumbies.

"See, my father did walk me down the aisle," she said, and smiled.

The Web site explains the process of creating the jewelry, which takes about four weeks. Costs range from $100 to $500.

So now I know just the gift I'll leave for my sister when I go.

MICHELLE'S FUNERAL ETIQUETTE

(Based on my own and my friends' experience)

1. The opening of a beer can during the service can be heard (the service tends to be quiet and you can hear the pop), so open it outside.
2. This is not the Indy; don't race the hearse to the burial.
3. Don't stand on other tombstones to get a better view.
4. The makeup is not for sale. Don't say the deceased looks way better than he or she ever did, and ask for the brand.
5. If it is a closed casket, don't ask, "How bad can it really be?" and lift the top for a look-see.
6. Doing funny impersonations of the deceased is never funny.
7. "Ripped off" should not come out of your mouth if you hear how much the funeral costs.
8. It is not polite to remove the earrings from the deceased, even if they are yours.
9. When you sign in, don't use a fake name like "Ima Hog."
10. Don't ask if the time was correctly printed in the paper because this is the smallest funeral you have ever been to.
11. If the deceased was a no-good cheating drunk, don't lie and tell the family he or she has gone to a better place.

BYE-BYE
BIRDIE

CHAPTER SIXTEEN

◎

The Nineteenth Hole

A guy comes home from golfing, and his wife asks him how it went.

"Well, we were doing fine until Bob had a heart attack and died on the fourth hole."

"Oh my God, that's terrible!"

"Yeah, you're telling me. For the rest of the afternoon, it was swing, drag Bob, swing, drag Bob . . ."

Golf enthusiasts, grab your travel bags. I have found a final resting place designed just for us. A place our friends will want to return to often . . . at least during golf season.

In Hickory, North Carolina, at Catawba Memorial Park, Chuck Gallagher has built a putting green that houses cremains.

Chuck, a golfer and a healthy forty-seven-year-old, is vice president of Stewart Enterprises, a New Orleans–based company founded in 1910 that owns and operates dozens of funeral homes and cemeteries around the country. Asked how he thought of such a fabulous concept as a memorial putting green—a stroke of genius, you might say—Chuck replies, "In our business, we're in a transition phase from the World War Two and Korean War generation to the baby boomers. We're finding that more and more of them want something different, unique, and distinctive."

Par for the course—baby boomers think differently from their parents. Chuck explains that boomers tend to look at death from a positive perspective, as a celebration, and "don't mind in any way, shape, or form being different. When they think about the experience at a cemetery, most of the time it's not perceived as being pleasant."

Forget the traditional image of a trip to the cemetery on a cold, gray day, the family gathered around Dad's mournful tombstone in the rain. At Catawba, Chuck says, "When the family returns they can bring their own putter and putt a ball into the hole."

In the soil beneath this putting green are ossuaries, containers that hold the cremains. Family and friends pour the remains of their loved ones into holes that lead down to these ossuaries. And if you decide to sink a putt during your visit, you needn't worry about losing your ball. The hole at the bottom of the cup is too small for the ball to pass through.

Just as there are many different clubs in a bag, Catawba

Memorial Park offers several choices for your remains. Around that special putting green there are cremation memorials. If you have a good short game, majestic oak trees stand just a sand wedge away, providing shady areas for scattering areas. A chip shot farther on, there's a fairway estate for people who prefer traditional burial. And if you take out your five-iron and hit a solid stroke, you can reach a mausoleum crypt for those who prefer aboveground entombment.

Like the pros traveling on tour, it doesn't matter where your home course might be—Catawba Memorial Park can be your fairway to heaven. The process is as simple as requesting a tee time; just place a call and make arrangements with Chuck. The required paperwork can be done by fax or FedEx, and survivors can either ship cremains or bring them.

Prices start at $500 for having your ashes deposited beneath the green. You also get your name on a bronze plaque at the site. At the high end of the price range, a private mausoleum for two in the fairway estate can run you $25,000.

"The purpose of a cemetery is not a repository for dead bodies," Chuck declares. "It's a place for people to return and remember those who have gone before them."

I suggest to him that for people choosing traditional burial, he might consider placing the ladies' graves twenty yards closer to the hole than the men's, and burying the men twenty yards ahead of the pros.

CHAPTER SEVENTEEN

◎

Super-Size Me

Take a quick look around the food court in your local mall, the people on either side of you on your next flight, the folks lying around you on the beach. Or just look in the mirror. We Americans are fat, and we're getting fatter.

Part of a widespread trend in this country to super-size everything from cars to toilet seats so that big Americans can fit into them, Goliath Casket of Lynn, Indiana, manufactures oversized caskets.

When I ask Goliath president, Keith Davis, how an in-the-box company developed such an outside-the-box idea, he laughs. "Have you been to Wal-Mart?" Then he adds, "Really, it was my father's idea."

In 1985, Keith's father, Forrest Davis, quit his job as a welder in a casket factory, where he had worked for more than thirty years. He came home and announced, "Boys, I'm gonna build oversized caskets that you would be proud to put your mother in."

The standard casket is 24 inches wide, measured "elbow to elbow," Keith explains. Goliath Casket began offering two sizes, 29 and 33 inches wide. In 1990, Keith and his wife, Julane, joined his father's business, and in 1994, when they took over, they expanded the product line—because one or two sizes do not fit all, even in the large-casket business.

Today, Goliath sizes include 29, 33, 35, 37, 40, 44, 48, and "the B-52 jumbo jet liner," Keith boasts. Just for perspective, that 52-inch casket is about the width of a Chevy S-10 pickup truck bed. "Actually, it won't quite fit inside the bed, but close," Keith notes. Goliath sold one B-52 a month in 2004. "That may not sound like a lot," Keith says, "but this niche market didn't even exist five years ago." With extra bracing and reinforced hinges and handles, these triple-wides are designed to handle bodies from 300 to a whopping 1,100 pounds.

Because times have changed along with our waistlines, Goliath also had to engineer the caskets to be deeper than standard. Keith, a normal-sized man, explains, "Oversized people are not just wide, they're thick. Trying to pick up the body just to get them into the casket is like picking up a water bed full of water." Sometimes, he says, the only way to lift a really big person into a casket is to rent the kind of hoist they use at the auto shop to lift engines.

With the casket weighing 250 pounds empty and the

occupant approaching 1,000 pounds, the next problem is how to move the casket. "One funeral home enlisted the aid of the local fire department," Keith tells me. "Another used a small front-end loader. All I can say is, be creative."

Keith notes other challenges with caskets this size, such as the need to obtain a double-sized vault, or the problem that an oversized casket may not fit through the doors of older funeral homes. "With a newer funeral home you have a better chance," he says.

Then there's the hearse. A standard hearse can't fit a casket more than thirty-six inches wide. A flat-bed truck or large van must be used instead. And then the oversized casket is taken to the cemetery, where the family has had to buy at least two grave plots to fit it.

Keith tells me that the family is rarely surprised to be going through all this. "The family has had to deal with this for years—they didn't just wake up one morning and find out that Mother weighs nine hundred pounds. They've had to have special chairs in the living room, special automobiles, special beds, everything."

Keith counsels the funeral home in the planning, helping them with things they may never have thought of. In some cases, for instance, all the body preparation, viewing, and services must be performed in a garage. "Decorated appropriately, it's fine. What isn't fine is finishing the service and the lid won't close because the body is too big."

All of Goliath's sales are through funeral homes or distributors, but a consumer can look at the casket options on the Web site. "We will work with a person, but we need to work with them through their funeral home," Keith explains. "It would be the same if you went out and bought a new steering wheel for your Cadillac and said, look at my new car. You only have one small part of the service."

Keith likes to say that Goliath is "the *Super-Size Me* of caskets." Sales "have been growing every year," he claims—and unfortunately, so have Americans.

GREEN SEED

Ecopod just might be the world's ultimate recycling program. This revolutionary coffin from the UK is made from naturally hardened, 100-percent-recycled paper.

A friend's death prompted designer Hazel Selena to investigate eco-friendly funerals and "green" burials. Seeking a new kind of coffin with a natural, organic shape, she began with an idea based on the seed pod, thinking of the deceased as a seed planted in the earth, bringing regeneration and new life. She added colors and patterns gleaned from her long interest in ancient Egyptian funerary art.

The handmade Ecopod, composed of pressed paper and glue, is totally biodegradable and quickly disintegrates in the ground with no harm to the environment. (And contrary to some ancient superstitions that are still with us, the decomposing body it held is good for the environment and poses no health threats.)

The British firm has filled orders from as far away as Mexico, at a cost of roughly $600 to $1,000.

CHAPTER EIGHTEEN

◎

Pushing Up Daisies

Physician Billy Campbell is one of the true visionaries of the eco-conscious "green burial" movement. A longtime environmentalist with an undergraduate degree in conservation biology to go along with his M.D., he founded Memorial Ecosystems and Ramsey Creek Preserve in South Carolina in 1996. It combines the functions of a memorial park and a nature preserve, saving acres of pristine woodland from development while providing a beautiful, totally natural setting for burials. For around $2,000 (or only $500 for cremated ashes), you can truly go back to nature when you die.

"The idea really came to me in middle school, when a teacher announced that when he died he wanted to be put in a burlap sack and have a tree planted over him," Dr. Campbell recalls. "I thought that was the coolest thing I had ever heard."

As both a baby boomer and a self-described "tree-huggin',

granola-eatin' hippie type," Dr. Campbell is perfectly in tune with the growing market for environmentally friendly burials. Think of green burial as a life-bracketing corollary to natural childbirth; it's "natural burial," without the embalming, the expensive caskets, the vaults, and all the other ecologically unsound practices common to traditional cemeteries. In green burial, no preservatives are used on the body, and all the burial materials, including the coffin and shroud, are biodegradable. The body as well as the burial materials decompose quickly and naturally, giving themselves back to nature and continuing the cycle of life. With green burial, you're literally pushing up daisies.

At Ramsey Creek, they don't even use headstones to mark the grave sites, which would interrupt the natural, wild beauty of the setting. Instead they place a flat rock or plant a bush to mark the site. And unlike traditional cemeteries, which crowd as many as one thousand graves into an acre of land, the density of grave sites is kept down to only around twenty-five per acre. Ultimately, Dr. Campbell says, he wants to encourage people to think of it not as "a cemetery" at all, but as a woodland area where they can hike, birdwatch, even hold weddings.

In the UK, where the green burial movement started, there are now more than 150 of these eco-conscious sites. The movement is just getting under way in the United States. Ramsey Creek was the first, though more are gradually being established around the country, and some conventional cemeteries are setting aside undeveloped acreage for similar use.

People from around the country are arranging to be buried at Dr. Campbell's South Carolina preserve, which was thirty-eight acres in 2005 with plans to increase it to three hundred. Only three states forbid the carting of unembalmed bodies across state lines, and Dr. Campbell argues this is only out of an archaic misconception that embalming somehow "sterilizes" the body and kills off all its germs, which is simply false. Most bodies that come to him from out of state are shipped by air in what are called "Ziegler containers," which keep the body cool so that it does not begin to decompose en route.

Dr. Campbell had conducted around one hundred burials as of 2005. His clients are not just fellow "hippie types," either. For instance, they have included a number of fundamentalist Christians, who see green burial as more in line with the Bible's "ashes to ashes, dust to dust" than contemporary cemetery practices that are geared to delay the body's natural decomposition.

Green burial represents another step in the evolution of contemporary attitudes toward birth and death. Not so long ago, few husbands would be present at the births of their children; sometimes the mother herself was so drugged that she was effectively not present, either. The whole miraculous process was left to professional strangers. Now both parents tend to participate in the joy of childbirth. At the other end of life's scale, the growing popularity of hospice care means that more people are dying naturally in their own homes now, surrounded by their loved ones, in a familiar and comforting setting, not surrounded by those professional strangers in an anonymous hospital ward full of terrifying machinery.

The green burial movement, like other practices described in this book, is an effort to make the passage from life to death more personal and connected with the rest of our lives. It reminds us that physical death and decay are natural processes, without which there could be no new life.

A F T E R W O R D

Before my son's precarious birth forced me to confront it, I didn't think much about death or funeral arrangements. Like a lot of folks, I suppose, death was just an inevitability I figured I'd deal with when the time came.

Then, as I met all these people taking charge of their exit strategies, I became curious about and eventually fascinated with death, all components of it. I don't mean that in a morbid sense. I didn't start dressing like Morticia Addams. But I did become very interested in all these options that are available to me—and you—when the time comes. I have decided, like the people in this book (and many, many others), that I want to have a say in what becomes of my remains. I would like it to be something socially beneficial; I don't want to waste land, money, or other resources.

And, of course, I want great wine and tequila and a fabulous band at the celebration.

I suppose a few people might see this book and think, "There go you boomers again. Still the 'me' generation. Still showing off and being 'different.' Even when you die you can't go quietly like everybody else. No, you have to turn yourselves into diamond rings, or go flying off to the moon, or get shot out of a cannon. Look at me, I'm a golf club! Still wasting money on your narcissistic wants and needs."

But if you've read this far into the book, I hope you've seen that the people I met weren't exploring these post-life options for selfish or silly reasons, and certainly are not throwing money around heedlessly. In almost all cases, the alternatives I describe in this book cost *less* than conventional funerals and burials—sometimes far less. Many of these options also conserve natural resources.

I think we're simplifying the process, even if we're doing that with our generation's characteristic flair for individual expression. One thing that struck me about this trend is that in a way it's actually old-fashioned. The funeral industry as we all think of it is really not much more than a century old. Before the twentieth century, from time immemorial, families and survivors were much more directly involved in the process. Most people died in their own homes and were laid out there (the origin of the term *funeral parlor*). Families and friends grieved together, made the final arrangements, and saw to it that the departed's last wishes were honored. It was only in relatively modern times that we gave that responsibility away to professionals—strangers who'd never met the deceased, or us.

Today, in increasing numbers, we're taking that responsibility back into our own hands. The funeral industry is scrambling to keep up with the changes. But more important, I think, death itself is changing. Death is becoming less the impersonal, terrifying stranger who knocks on our door in the middle of the night and carts us away into the darkness. Now it's a ride in a balloon. Or a fireworks display. Or a trip to the moon. Or being turned into a lovely diamond. Or a chance to give something back to Mother Nature and participate in the great cycle of being.

Those are all so much more positive, hopeful, and sane ways of thinking about it. Maybe that's why I met so many wonderful people as I researched this topic. Even in one of the saddest moments of their lives, they were warm and open to me. I learned so much from them. Through this book I've tried to pass the best—and the most interesting—of what I learned along to you.

RESOURCES

Ash-Scattering Services

Aerial Missions
Jim and Wendy Howard
10721 25th Avenue SW
Seattle, WA 98146
Phone: (206) 409-0229
Web site: www.aerialmissions.com

Aloha Scattering Service
23 Mikiola Street, No. A
Makawao, HI 96768
Phone: (808) 573-3494
Web site: http://alohascattering.com
Professional ash-scattering service on Maui. Offers ocean and mountain services and pet-ash scattering.

Angel Air Nationwide Ash
Scattering Service
P.O. Box 1109
415 West First Avenue
Big Timber, MT 59011
Phone: (406) 932-6877
Web site: www.angelair.net
The only nationwide professional ash-scattering service.

Atlantis Memorials
Sausalito, CA 94965
Phone: (415) 332-3291
Fax: (415) 331-7091
Web site: www.atlantismemorials.com
Offers professional scattering of cremains at sea from yachts on San Francisco Bay and near the Golden Gate Bridge.

Atlantis Society
3408 Via Oporto
Suite 206
Newport Beach, CA 92663
Phone: (949) 300-8888
Web site: www.atlantissociety.com
*Maritime funeral service providers,
serving California and Washington
state.*

Burial at Sea Services
Captain Jay Murphy
Key West, Florida
Phone: (305) 292-1478
Web site: www.buryatsea.com

Cape Cod Burials at Sea
Web site:
www.capecodboattours.com/ccbas
*Offers ash scattering, burials at sea,
and memorial charters off Cape Cod,
using a former U.S. Navy vessel.
USCG-licensed crew and certified vessel operate year-round.*

Cloud 9 Coastal Flights
John Thomas Rethke
King City, CA 93930
Phone: (831) 385-5942
Web site: www.cloud9flights.com
*Aerial dispersion of cremated remains
off California's Big Sur coastline.*

Four Winds Aerial Services
Division of R. L. Carmichael
    and Assoc., Inc.
3102B Tyre Neck Road
Portsmouth, VA 23703
Phone: (757) 465-5600
Web site: www.fourwindsaerial.com
*Flights over the Atlantic near Chesa-
peake Bay.*

A Journey with Wings
Phone: (800) 407-6401
Web site:
www.ajourneywithwings.com
*Southern California aerial scattering
service.*

The Neptune Society, Inc.
Web site: www.neptunesociety.com
*Comprehensive cremation and sea scat-
tering services for California, Florida,
New York, Oregon, Washington,
Iowa, and Arizona.*

Ecologically Sound Alternatives

Ecopod
Anne Nightingale, Sales Director
91 Western Road, Unit 7
Brighton, East Sussex BN1 2NW
United Kingdom
Phone: (44) (0) 1273 746011
Fax: (44) (0) 1273 734160
E-mail: anne@eco-pod.com
Web site: www.eco-pod.co.uk

Forever Fernwood
301 Tennessee Valley Road
Mill Valley, CA 94941
Phone: (415) 383-7100
Fax: (415) 383-7409
E-mail:
webmaster@forevernetwork.com
Web site: www.foreverfernwood.com

Glendale Memorial Nature Preserve
297 Railroad Avenue
DeFuniak Springs, FL 32433
Phone: (850) 859-2141
E-mail:
info@glendalenaturepreserve.org
Web site:
www.glendalenaturepreserve.org

Memorial Ecosystems and Ramsey
Creek Preserve
Dr. Billy Campbell
111 West Main Street
Westminster, SC 29693
Tel: (864) 647-7798
Fax: (864) 647-0403
E-mail:
kimberly@memorialecosystems.com
Web site:
www.memorialecosystems.com

Other Services

Alcor Life Extension Foundation
Joseph Waynick
7895 East Acoma Drive, Suite 110
Scottsdale, AZ 85260
Phone: (480) 905-1906
Fax: (480) 922-9027
Toll-free: (877) 462-5267
E-mail: jennifer@alcor.org
Web site: www.alcor.org

Beth Menczer Pottery
P.O. Box 267
Glenwood, NM 88039
Phone: (505) 539-2373
E-mail: menczer4@yahoo.com
Web site: beth.menczer.com

Catawba Memorial Park
Chuck Gallagher
3010 Highway 70 SE
Hickory, NC 28603
Phone: (828) 322-8646
Fax: (828) 244-1400
E-mail: cgallagher@stei.com

Celebration Forest
Heidi E. Stockton
9728 Colburn Culver Road
Sandpoint, ID 83864
Phone: (877) 245-7378
Fax: (208) 267-4306
E-mail: info@celebrationforest.com
Web site: www.celebrationforest.com

Companion Star Crystal
and Memorials
Phyllis Janik
P.O. Box 423
Hinsdale, IL 60522-0423
Phone: (630) 561-1850
E-mail: lily@companionstar.com
Web site: www.companionstar.com

Creative Cremains
David Riccomi
Rena Fregosi
1775 Egbert Avenue
San Francisco, CA 94124
Phone: (415) 468-6044
Fax: (415) 468-5674
E-mail: info@creativecremains.com
Web site: www.creativecremains.com

The Eternal Ascent Society
Joanie West
8395 Yew Pine Court
Crystal River, FL 34428
Phone: (352) 563-5266
Toll-free: (800) 808-2082
Web site: www.eternalascent.com

Eternal Reefs, Inc.
Don Brawley
P.O. Box 2473
Decatur, GA 30031
Phone: (888) 423-7333
E-mail: info@eternalreefs.com
Web site: www.eternalreefs.com

Goliath Casket, Inc.
Keith and Julane Davis
8261 S. 350 East
Lynn, IN 47355
Phone: (765) 874-2380
Fax: (765) 874-1944
Web site: www.oversizecasket.com

LifeGem
Rusty VandenBiesen
836 Arlington Heights Road, #311
Elk Grove Village, IL 60007
Phone: (866) 543-3436
E-mail: info@lifegem.com
Web site: www.lifegem.com

Madelyn Company
Joni G. Cullen
Lisa Saxer-Buros
2811 Milton Avenue, Suite 400
Janesville, WI 53545
Phone: (800) 788-0807
Fax: (608) 752-3683
E-mail: madelynco@charter.net
Web site:
www.madelynpendants.com
*Contact your local funeral director or a
local distributor for styles and prices.*

MHP Enterprises
RR #1, S-7, C-7
Crescent Valley
British Columbia V0G 1H0
Canada
Phone: (800) 789-9395
E-mail: mhp@casketfurniture.com
Web site: www.casketfurniture.com

Summum
Corky Ra
707 Genesee Avenue
Salt Lake City, UT 84104
Phone: (801) 355-0137
E-mail:
mummification@summum.org
Web site: www.summum.org

Space Services Inc.
Charles Chafer
2476 Bolsover, Suite 415
Houston, TX 77005
Phone: (281) 971-4019
E-mail:
contact@spaceservicesinc.com
Web site: www.spaceservicesinc.com

Thumbies Keepsake Pendants
Meadow Hill Company, Inc.
405 Midway Street
Fox Grove, IL 60021
Phone: (877) 848-6243
Fax: (847) 462-0703
E-mail: info@thumbies.com
Web site: www.goldthumbprints.com

Michelle Cromer has worked in marketing and advertising for more than twenty-five years and is a partner at Sanders Wingo Advertising, located in Austin and El Paso, Texas. She is the founder of Pink Crosses, a foundation for the families of the more than three hundred women who have been murdered over the past decade in Juárez, Mexico. Michelle lives in El Paso and Ruidoso, New Mexico, with her husband and their two sons.

CORE COLLECTION 2006